How to Quit Your Job
with
Rental Properties

A Step-by-Step Guide to
Retire Early with
*Real Estate Investing
and Passive Income*

EXPANDED AND UPDATED

DUSTIN HEINER

"Ninety percent of all millionaires became so through owning real estate." – Andrew Carnegie

ISBN-13: 978-1-946965-07-3

DEDICATION

To my lovely bride Melissa and my amazing children Ellie, Elias, Xander, and Faith, without you, none of this would matter. Thank you for being my inspiration and motivation.

To the Lord Jesus Christ who makes all things possible and who loves me and gave Himself up for me.

CONTENTS

DOWNLOAD THE FREE ACTION GUIDE AND OTHER GREAT RESOURCES TODAY!

We've found that readers have the most success with our book when they use the Action Guide as they read. Just to say thank you for buying this book, we'd like to give you the full Action Guide and other great resources **100% FREE**

DOWNLOAD FREE INSTANTLY HERE

http://www.masterpassiveincome.com/free-action-guide

PHASE 1

BLUEPRINT AND PLANNING

PHASE 1.1

GROUNDWORK FOR FINANCIAL INDEPENDENCE

"Ninety percent of all millionaires
became so through owning real estate.

- Andrew Carnegie

The walk to my car after work on December 15th, 2016 was the best walk I ever took. As I left my job for the final time, with all my family pictures, including one of a painted red lobster that my two year old daughter made, and personal items in tow, I couldn't help but think that I was very blessed.

Now I can do whatever I want, whenever I want, and never answer to a boss again!

You know, on that beautiful rainy walk to my car, I couldn't help but think how all this was possible. Looking back over the past years of my life building my passive income businesses, it was all worth it.

All the sacrifices, hard times, ups-and-downs of the passive income business life was absolutely worth it. I am proof that this passive income thing really works! At age 37, I quit my job and will NEVER work a job again! And this is all thanks to passive income and the businesses I have created.

This is what I want to happen for you. I want to see your life change as I have seen with so many of my real estate investing students. It took me 9 years to finally quit my job with rental properties. Some of my students have quit their jobs in half the time.

I want to congratulate you for deciding to change your financial future and create your own financial independence. Get ready to join a huge list of successfully unemployed real estate investors in quitting their job and living the dream life.

This is going to be exciting, challenging, and very informative for you to start your investing business. By the time you reach the end of this book, you are going to be absolutely ready to start your investing business in rental properties.

As you go through the phases in this book, you will see that it is specifically designed for you to learn how to build your financial freedom in real estate rental properties from the ground up. It is designed with five separate phases that build on top of each other. After each chapter, you will have action items for you to complete.

It is very important that you complete each action item before you move on to the next chapter. Each chapter will build on itself and it would be best not to put anything off and miss important keys to your success. I completely understand the desire to skip ahead to read the section that interest you the most or applies to where you are right now.

Think of it this way: If you didn't know how to fly a plane, would it be wise to get in the cockpit, start the engine, and try to fly? By trying to fly without learning how to do it would be crazy and dangerous. Investing without learning the business would be like me giving you the keys to the plane but not the knowledge or understanding of how to do it.

Resist the temptation to skip ahead because there is a process to learn the steps to build a successful business. You don't want to miss anything that could be crucial to a successful business. Even more, you don't want to miss something that could cost you thousands of dollars in your business because you didn't build the business the right way.

With rental properties, your life will be changed. Instead of crashing in burning, you want to be at the top of the world flying over everyone. So picture yourself, after learning the skills and attaining the knowledge of the business, soaring way above the clouds living the dream life.

Stop and ask yourself these questions:

How would my life be if:

- I did not need to work 40+ hours a week for someone else in order to make money to pay my bills?
- I never had to worry about how to pay my bills again?
- I could design my life the way I want to live it instead of designing my life around my job?
- I had all the time in the world to exercise, serve the community, or take up that hobby you have been putting off for years.?
- I could live anywhere in the world because money doesn't matter and I wasn't stuck working a J.O.B.?

These are all the questions the financially rich people of the world have the ability to actually ask themselves. This is because they do not work for money anymore. They have their money work for them. This is the key principle of passive income.

Let's look at that one more time. Have your money work for you instead of you working for your money. It sounds easy doesn't it? While it is not truly easy, it is truly simple. I say it is simple because of how little time I spend on my business and how I make ridiculous amounts of money without even working. This is what I want to teach you.

Once you learn from those who have already designed their life to fit them, not their job, you will see how truly simple it is. Those people have found the amazing blessings of real estate rental properties. After spending 9 years building a successful real estate business, I am able to live the life of my dreams.

Let me give you an example: I spend 3 hours, at most, buying one property. Once I own the property, I have others do the work for me like fixing it up, getting it rented, collecting rents, maintain the property, etc. From those 3 hours of work, I make money every day until I sell the property.

This is how I am able to travel the world for weeks at a time. In 2018, I took my wife and four children on a 6 week vacation seeing 11 countries. In that same year, I went on a guy's fishing trip in Alaska for 2-weeks. In 2017, I drove my family 1200 miles around Japan for 6 weeks. What I have done is build a business where I have other people work for me and I reap all the benefits.

To get started, you need to learn how to think like those who are already rich. By educating yourself about how to use your money to work for you, you will have the ability to design your life the way you want it to be. You can design your life around you, not around your job.

In order to understand what passive income through rental properties is, it would be good to understand how you can make income. There are two ways to earn income:

■ Earned Income: Includes all the taxable income and wages you get from employment. i.e. working a J.O.B. (Just Over Broke) and trading hours for dollars.

■ Passive Income: Income received on a regular basis, with little effort required to maintain it. For example, you get paid for the value that you bring, not for the hours that you work.

WHAT TO EXPECT IN THIS BOOK

In this book there are five Phases you will be going through. Each phase builds upon itself just like a home you are going to buy as a rental.

Phase 1 is the Blueprint and Planning section of the learning process. A blueprint is the instructions on how to build a house from the ground up. Just like having instructions on how to build a house, you need to have instructions on how to invest properly and not lose money.

Phase 1 will help you see the blueprint that you need to follow in order to replace your income with rental properties so you can quit your job and live the good life.

Phase 2, you will be going through the "foundations" of passive income investing. This is where you will build your future financial freedom in real estate rental properties. Like the foundation of a building, your passive income investing foundation must be deep, solid, and strong. The foundation must be poured, cured, and set before you start to build the structure of your business.

The work done in this phase will set the course for the rest of your life. Take the foundations very seriously and put in the work necessary to build a super solid foundation. In it you will learn about yourself, rental properties, and how the rich use real estate to create massive amounts of wealth, passive income, and financial freedom.

Phase 3 is the "structure" section. The structure you build, which sits on top of the foundation, is the frame of the business. This is the section that holds everything together and keeps the building from falling in on itself.

With a strong structure, there will not be many things that will bring your building down because the structure is secure and sound. In this section, you will learn how you can quit your J.O.B. (Just Over Broke) and live off of the passive income you bring in through rental properties.

Phase 4 is the "finishing touch" section. In this section, you will focus on the details of your business and how to implement your business properly. The finishing touches are what everyone sees, admires, and wants to be a part of.

When your business is like a well-built structure, you will be able to get through everything that comes in your way. With this section you will learn how to get to work on building your business for financial success.

Phase 5 is the section where you are given specific steps and action items to get started. If you follow these steps, it will not be a matter of "if" but "when" you get your first property. Be sure to follow each step because they are proven to work. If you are diligent and patient, you will have your first rental property within a couple months.

Remember, this is a working book, so it is designed to challenge you and help you on the path to financial freedom with rental properties. There will be a lot to learn, but you must push through each day and do the daily action items if you want to truly be able to quit your job.

How You Can Master Passive Income

Passive income is making money by the things you "own" or

"create." The goal is to replace your income with an income that comes in whether they do any work or not. Passive income allows you to get paid by the value you bring, not the hours you put in.

If you have $3,500 in personal expenses per month, and your monthly passive income from your rental properties is $4,000 a month, then you do not need to work a job any more. Your personal expenses are now covered by your real estate business.

You can now quit your job and design your life the way you want to live it. The secret to being rich is to spend your time and money acquiring businesses, real estate, intellectual property, inventions, etc. that will make you money even when you do not work.

These are things that bring in money every month for you and your family to live. There are many different types of passive income streams, but the way the rich make their money is by owning real estate that generates monthly cash flow.

Passive Income = The Less You Work, The More Money You Make

The principles of passive income are simple and seem easy to do. That is the beauty of the master passive income business model. Implementing these principles into your business will allow you to change your life and never work a J.O.B. again.

With passive income, the goal is to get paid for the value that you bring, not the hours that you work. Stop trading hours for dollars. That is what people with a poor mindset do.

Having a business in real estate rental properties you work hard in the beginning setting up the company, buying properties, and get them rented. After you have done all the work in the beginning, you let your systems take over, and the business makes money for you even if you do not work.

Mastering Passive Income

More millionaires are made from real estate than any other means of wealth creation. You can master the game of life if you master passive income.

Here is how you do it: Build a real estate business that passively increases wealth, brings in monthly cash flow, and allows you to quit your J.O.B. through rental properties and real estate investing.

Have you ever wonder why the rich keep getting richer? The reason is simple. It is because they let their money work for them rather than working for money.

Ninety percent of the rich keep their money in real estate. Not only do they keep their money in real estate but they keep making more money from the real estate that they own.

BUILD A REAL ESTATE BUSINESS THAT PASSIVELY INCREASES WEALTH, BRINGS IN MONTHLY CASH FLOW, AND ALLOWS YOU TO QUIT YOUR J.O.B. THROUGH RENTAL PROPERTIES AND REAL ESTATE INVESTING.

In America, the laws are not made to only benefit those who are rich since we have equal justice under the law, but the laws apply to you and me the same as they apply to the rich. The difference is the rich know how to use the laws in their favor to make more money, and you can learn how, too!

Will This Work in Places Outside America?

I have many students who do not live in America and they are also investing in real estate. The most common question I get from students who live outside the United States is, "Can I invest in real estate in my country?"

The simple answer is: "Absolutely, yes"!

As long as a person is able to own property without the government or others taking it away from them, then they will have the ability to invest in real estate. There are principles that an investor must follow if they are to be successful.

In Phase 3 of this book, I will give you the principles you need to invest in real estate anywhere in the world.

What Passive Income is Not

It is not trading hours for dollars. When you have a job, you put in an hour of work and get an hour's worth of wages in return. If you don't work, you don't get paid. Working a job is an example of trading hours for dollars, and it is not how the rich do it.

Being a sole proprietor of any type of business is not a passive source of income. If you don't service your customers you don't get paid. You have substituted one boss for many different ones that can fire you whenever they want.

For years, we have all been educated in the public school system and taught how to be an employee where we trade hours for dollars. It's time to learn a new way of making money for yourself and your family.

You need to learn the strategy and tactics the rich use to create wealth, keep their wealth, and create even more wealth. It will take hard work, perseverance, dedication, and passion if you want to make passive income as the rich do with rental properties.

It does not happen quickly, nor is it a get rich quick scheme. This is a get wealth plan. The principle of the rich is they use their money to make more money. You may be starting out with very little to no money, but that shouldn't stop you, nor should it stop you that you don't know how to even get started. I did not let that stop me from starting, and you shouldn't either.

Real Estate Investing Is Not A Get Rich Quick Scheme

It Is A Get Wealthy Plan

PHASE 1.2

CASE STUDY:
$9,600 A Month Profit From Rental Properties

I couldn't help but laugh.

"I didn't know you were that rich." Matt, a friend of mine said to me one day.

"What?" I replied

"You are quitting your job, you have to be rich!" He added.

"I'm not rich... Well, it all depends on what you consider to be rich. " I said as I chuckled a bit.

"I think someone is rich when they have millions of dollars and can buy whatever they want" he explained.

"Well, by that standard, I'm not rich. What is interesting though is that you don't have to be rich to quit your job," I said as I paused to read the expression on his face. "You just need to make enough passive income to replace your earned income."

He looked a little puzzled as the thought of my quitting quickly sank in.

"No," I continued. "I am not rich but I have all my needs met with my rental properties and online businesses that I do not need to work. It has taken me nine years to get to this point and I am ready to quit."

"What do you mean you have all your needs met?" he asked.

"Well, my businesses bring in money in the form of cash flow each month. That means that each month, I have money put into my pocket from my businesses. I have built up my businesses enough that the income each month has surpassed the income from my job."

"So, your rental properties bring in rent and your online businesses bring in money from advertising and sales?" he asked as he was starting to understand.

"Correct! There are ups and downs in sales and rent amount each month but on average, all my expenses are paid for by my businesses. I am quitting my job, not because I'm rich, but because I can," I said.

As we sat in the waiting room of a large hospital to see my best friend who was fighting for his life, I went further into detail on two things; the "How" and the "Why" of me quitting my job. You see, he believed that only rich people did not have jobs. Well, I guess if that is the definition of being rich, then I am truly rich.

Some people desire to have expensive cars, fancy homes and a lavish lifestyle. Those things are fine for some, but that is not what I desired when I made the commitment to myself to quit my job. I wanted the ability to no longer work for someone else and spend more time with my amazing wife and beautiful children.

I also wanted to have the freedom to do the things I wanted to do. So, yes, I most definitely am rich by those standards and I agree. Honestly, this is what my entire goal was 9 years prior, to be independent and not have to work for anyone.

What I explained to Matt was that the "Why" was just as important as the "How" in anything and especially when it came to quitting your job. If you don't know why you desire to quit your job, how will you know when it is the right time to quit? Some people make money their passion. The end goal is the money itself. The problem with having money be your passion is that you get to become just like J.D. Rockefeller, one of the richest men in history.

When he was asked the question "How much money is enough?" his answer was very telling of his passion for money, "Just a little bit more." The desire for money never stops, but can actually become your master if you let it. As you pursue it, it will always flee from you.

I find it is best to use it as a tool for the more important things in life. On my death bed, I would regret the time I wasted chasing after things that were not important. What is important is my Lord, my wife, my children, my family, and my friends.

> I WANTED THE ABILITY TO NO LONGER WORK FOR SOMEONE ELSE AND SPEND MORE TIME WITH MY FAMILY WHILE DOING THE THINGS I WANT TO DO.

Rental properties allowed me to replace my income from my job in four years with a monthly passive income, and you can, too. How I started is probably similar to how you are starting: no money, decent credit, and the desire to learn how I can make money from rental properties.

Taking our wedding money, I spent $1,000 on a 2-day

training course with a real estate "guru" in order to learn how to invest in real estate. The course was a very broad overview of real estate investing, and it had so much information that it was like drinking water out of the fire hose.

The seminar had information on every type of real estate investing there is. Wholesaling, Flipping, Land Contracts, Rental Properties, Tax Liens, etc. This was good information but it was just an overview with nothing to really implement. The content was so broad that it made you feel like you needed to spend the $30,000 for their full course.

After the two-day seminar the "guru" made a sales pitch for $30,000 more for a week-long course in Florida. I thought that was crazy; not to mention that I didn't have $30,000. Even if I did have $30,000, I wanted to use that money on buying a rental property.

The one good thing about that seminar was that it got me started down the path of investing in real estate. After taking the course, I made the conscious decision to become an investor in real estate rental properties. So, I set off on my own path educating myself with everything I could get my hands on.

The first priority was to educate myself with books, courses, and audio books. The quickest way for me to learn was to get practical experiences in real estate while buying my first property. While I don't suggest this now, I took the school of hard knocks to learn real estate investing.

Looking back now, I lost so much money because I didn't know what I was doing. Literally tens of thousands of dollars from missed problems with properties, property managers stealing from me, evictions, not screening tenants properly, etc. All of these things could have been avoided if I took a real estate course.

But! That $30,000 course was just way too much. If I would have found a course that was $5,000, I would probably have taken it. Looking back now, I would tell my younger investing self to find a mentor or take an online course that would help me start and run a successful real estate business.

There are many lessons that I learned the hard way that I have incorporated into my investing business which helps me to be a better investor. These good and bad experiences have helped me to develop and hone my skills in rental property investing. Now I make 5 times as much as I did from my job in passive income.

To get started, I needed to figure out what it would take for me to retire from my job by objectively looking at my income AND expenses. By knowing what my expenses were, I was able to have a target income to hit if I would ever be able quit my job.

To do that, I completed a budget for my family (like one you will be doing in this book), and that gave me the total dollar amount that I needed in order to live life without my job. The total I needed was $4,000 a month from passive income for my family to live securely without my job.

To get started, I took our savings of $17,000 and bought one property in Ohio (even though I lived in California) that cash flowed $350 per month. Each time I received a rent check, I saved the profit for future investing. I then took out a small loan on the first property and bought two more properties that brought in a total of $600 a month for both.

Now, my passive income from rental properties was a total of $950 per month with just three properties in one year! From there, I saved as much of the profits as I could and continued to buy at least three properties each year.

After 8 years, I owned 18 homes that rented for $500 a month which is $9,000 in rent per month! After expenses, the check I receive in my mailbox, for not doing any work myself, is right around $6,500. I had successfully surpassed my income of $4,000 per month and an extra $2,500 per month!

Here is the timeline for how I bought my first 19 properties:

- ❖ July 2007: Property 1
    - ○ Cash price $17,000 – Rents for $525
    - ○ Refinanced the property and took out $15,000 to buy my second property.
- ❖ October 2007: Property 2
    - ○ Cash price $10,200 – Rents for $550
    - ○ Refinanced the property and took out $20,000 to buy two more properties.
- ❖ April 2008: Property 3
    - ○ Cash price $10,000 – Rents for $500
    - ○ June 2008: Property 4
    - ○ Cash price $7,500 – Rents for $500

In real estate, buying properties with creative financing is one strategy to grow the business fast. One creative way to get financing is to use a credit card to purchase a property. You may say to me, "That is crazy risky!" Sure, it would be crazy if you were getting a 21% interest rate on the loan! It would also be crazy if you didn't know what you were doing.

The credit card I took advantage of was a cash out offer of 1.50% interest rate for the life of the loan. Think about it. A regular loan would be at least 4% interest for the life of the loan. With this credit card, I would only be paying 1.5%! Even with the different way credit cards calculate interest, this was a huge win!

With a credit limit of $14,000, I pulled out every penny I could to purchase the next property. This next property brought in $525 a month in rent. Since the interest on the credit was only $50 a month, I was ahead $475! Talk about a great loan!

- ❖ September 2008: Property 5
    - ○ Cash price $13,000 – Rents for $525
- ❖ September 2008: Property 6
    - ○ Cash price $6,500 – Rents for $500
- ❖ October 2008: Property 7

- o Cash price $6,500 – Rents for $500
- ❖ March 2010: Property 8
  - o Cash price $7,800 – Rents for $500
- ❖ July 2010: Property 9
  - o Cash price $9,200 – Rents for $525
- ❖ May 2011: Property 10
  - o Cash price $10,500 – Rents for $525
- ❖ June 2011: Property 11
  - o Cash price $9,000 – Rents for $500
- ❖ July 2011: Property 12 & 13 (Duplex)
  - o Cash price $12,000 – Rents for $850
- ❖ February 2012: Property 14
  - o Cash price $8,900 – Rents for $525
- ❖ April 2013: Property 15
  - o Cash price $11,000 – Rents for $525
- ❖ February 2013: Property 16
  - o Cash price $7,800 – Rents for $525
- ❖ March 2013: Property 17
  - o Cash price $8,200 – Rents for $495
- ❖ December 2013: Property 18
  - o Cash price $8,900 – Rents for $525
- ❖ November 2015: Property 19
  - o Cash price $9,000 – Rents for $495

The total rental income, not including expenses, for these properties each month is: $9,590! Not too bad for 8 years of investing! Building up a business that has 19 properties took hard work, sacrifice, and dedication.

Since 2015, I have continued to build my rental business to even more properties and passive income in the form of monthly cash flow. Each property I buy brings in more money for me to buy more properties, which brings in more money so I can buy more properties and so on. I will never stop buying properties.

In December 2016, I worked my last day at a job ever. Because I pushed hard for 9 years, I am blessed to have quit my job and never have to work again.

Honestly, this is not *rocket science*, nor is it something that you cannot do. It is something that anybody can do as long as they learn how to play the game like the rich play it. The laws are designed to make you rich with passive income in rental properties. Just by reading this book you are way ahead of me when I started and will learn from my mistakes.

You are on your path to financial freedom with rental properties in real estate.

GET PAID WHAT YOU ARE WORTH

You are worth more money than an hourly wage that you could earn from any job. I know that sounds crazy to hear but it's true. Since elementary school, we have all been trained to work day-in and day-out at a job to make money to support ourselves.

The reality is that you can make so much more money on your own than you ever could working for someone else. No matter what job you have, or how much you make per hour, you are worth much more than that. If you really think about it, the hourly wage you are paid shows how much our employer believes we are worth.

If you have a minimum wage job, you are only worth that to your employer. If your hourly wage is $100 an hour, then that is exactly how much you are worth. I'm here to tell you that you are worth much more than ANYONE can pay you. What you are being paid is not a true reflection of what you are worth.

Your time should not be valued in dollars and cents. What you are worth is the value that you bring to anything that you do and whatever you apply yourself to. When you accept an hourly wage, you are agreeing with your employer on how much your time and talents are worth.

You are worth more than the paycheck you receive every two weeks. The value that you bring to your business is worth much more than any amount of money you can make per hour. All you need to do is realize that when your employer is paying you for your hour, he is really paying you to do something that will make him more money.

Why not employ yourself and make 100% of the money from the time you spend working? Why shouldn't it be YOU who profits from your hard work and life spent building something? I'm telling you that there is no reason why YOU couldn't be the business owner, the investor, or the entrepreneur who makes money from your time spent doing work on your own business.

THREE AMAZING THINGS PASSIVE INCOME RENTAL PROPERTIES ALLOWS YOU TO HAVE

There are three things that the rich have in abundance that most do not. Those who are educated as the rich are can have these three things in abundance too.

Think what your life would be like if you did not have to work for a mortgage/rent, car payment, insurance, bills, etc. If you were able to bring in enough money to pay all your expenses without working a single day, you would be among those that are truly rich.

MONEY

Having passive income means having money to spend on whatever you want. Feel like buying a Porsche? Want to ski in the Alps with your five closest friends? Want a 5000 square foot home? All of these are possible for the rich because they have the money to do so. For the Porsche, the rich do not go out and buy a Porsche and pay cash.

They buy an investment that brings in enough money each month to pay for the Porsche's monthly payment. Once the

Porsche is paid off, the rich person owns the Porsche AND the investment that bought the Porsche which continues to bring in passive income year after year.

What would my hourly rate be for working two hours to buy one rental property that brings me $300 of monthly cash flow for years and years to come? The number is almost unquantifiable since the money created from my two hours of work will always be working for me. Not until I decide to sell the property and cash out would you be able to find my hourly rate.

However, I do not believe I would ever cash out, but instead, do a 1031 exchange and purchase a property that brings me even more monthly cash flow. Even if I decide to sell the property and move the money into a better property, my original two hours gained me money from the property appreciating, and that money is still working for me in a new property that makes me more money.

TIME

The most expensive thing you can spend is your time. What and who you spend it on is your choice but with a J.O.B. (Just Over Broke), you are forced to spend 40 hours of your 168 hours a week working for a paycheck.

There are not many people who want to spend their time working for someone else. You can be certain the rich do not want to spend their time doing that. Passive income in rental properties gives you time to do whatever you want, whenever you want.

Want to take a two-month backpacking trip through the John Muir Trail in the Sierra Nevada Mountains? Or walk through Jerusalem, Bethlehem, and visit the garden of Gethsemane, all while being paid at the same time? Passive income from rental properties allows you to spend an indefinite amount of time doing what you choose to do, whenever you want to do it.

Through buying investments that bring in passive income each month, you will not have to work a J.O.B. ever again. When you are working a J.O.B. you are trading dollars for hours. The rich do not get paid by the hours they work but on the value they produce.

Instead of working more hours, or trying to find a job that pays more, the rich buy more things that bring them money each month passively. When I buy a rental property, I work only about two hours on a deal from beginning to end and have money coming in for the rest of my life from that one property. The property managers, contractors, inspectors, etc., do all the work for me. I pay them well because I don't want to do the work, and they are more than willing to do it for me.

CONTROL

Master passive income gives you control over the things that bring in passive income and does not leave it up to chance, or someone else, to make their investment increase. When you buy a stock in a publicly traded company, you are buying into the profits and losses of that company.

You, as a small shareholder in the company, have no say on what the business does or does not do. When you invest in rental properties, you control every aspect of the property and business.

Unlike stocks, where you have no control over the business, you have complete control over your real estate business. Want to increase rents? Increase the value of the property, and the customers will pay more to live there.

Need to replace an AC unit and want to save money by buying a smaller unit because the original was too big? That is your choice. Want to pass on a tenant that has bad credit and prior evictions? Again, these are all in your control. You have complete control over the business and property to do as you see fit.

When you purchase properties as rentals, the best way to go is to "control" the property and not own them. You may buy your personal residence in your name, but the investment properties should be put into a company you create, like an LLC. An LLC is a Limited Liability Company that you own and control, and the LLC then owns the property.

Since it is the LLC that owns the property and not you personally, if the property ever gets sued, you are not personally liable with your assets safe. Remember that you "control" the property; you do not own it.

Think far ahead, past your next few paychecks, to your retirement. What happens when you no longer are able to work for money because of old age? You may say, "I will have Social Security, a 401k, an IRA, a pension plan from my work, or even a nest egg saved up." All of these things are good in theory, but this is not how the rich make their money.

You can say, "My money is working for me in my IRA or savings account." Sure. But the return is too low, you have no control, and it doesn't give you the ability to make enough money to design your life the way you want it.

I am so excited for you and the new journey you are on with passive income in real estate with rental properties. This book will take you step-by-step through the process of going from no properties to 20, 50, or even 300 properties.

The sky is the limit for you and it only depends on how big you want to grow your business. Once you are done with this book, you will have the knowledge to create the income a rock star like you deserves!

PHASE 1.3

FOUR STAGES OF
REAL ESTATE INVESTING

When it comes to learning how to invest in real estate rental properties, you may encounter some negative people. People that tell you that real estate investing is risky and how you will lose money doing it. These nay-sayers will try to keep you back from greatness. Keep you back from living the dream life.

It is important that you understand the four stages of competence in your life to know where you are and how you can get to the next stage in your real estate investing business. The only way to master anything is to progress through each stage to the fourth stage where you have mastered your skill or craft.

Every investor goes through all of these stages. The key is to continue progressing through these stages until you have made it to the final stage. Mastery.

Let's go through the four stages and break them down piece by piece so you can understand your journey with investing in real estate.

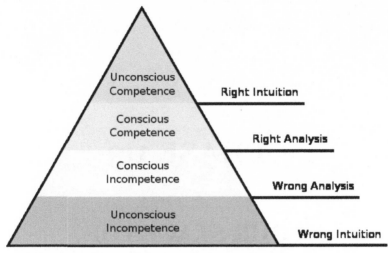

Hierarchy of Competence

Unconscious Incompetence

The person in this phase does not understand or know how to do something or know that "something" actually exists. The saying "You don't know what you don't know" applies to the people in this stage. It can even be that the person knows what they don't know but chooses to stay ignorant of the skill.

To move past this stage, the person must recognize their own incompetence as well as value the new skill before moving on to the next stage. One can move past this stage more quickly with the desire to learn and willingness to spend the time developing the new skill.

Conscious Incompetence

In this stage, knowledge of the skills existence and the understanding of its necessity is recognized but the ability to carry out the skill is lacking. Once the individual knows they are missing something in their skill set, they can put forth the effort to learn the skill.

When learning the new skill, as in learning anything, trial and error will take place. Failure will lead to success as the individual continues to train and learn the new skill.

Conscious Competence

The individual in this stage understands the skill and is able to apply the skill with limited failure. Even though they know the new skill, it takes the individual to have considerable concentration to perform the skill well.

The skill may be broken down into smaller steps to make the task or skill easier to manage. It takes conscious effort to execute this new skill and apply the right actions to be successful.

Unconscious Competence

This individual has had so much practice with the new skill that it becomes second nature and can be performed easily and with limited concentration. One can even perform another task at the same time because of muscle memory, complete knowledge, and practical experience with the skill.

"If you can't explain it to a six-year-old, you don't understand it yourself." –Albert Einstein

Think of professionals who have played their sport for 5, 10, or 15 years perfecting their skills. Professionals like Michael Jordan, Lebron James, Tom Brady, Tiger Woods, Warren Buffet, Bill Gates, Jim Rogers, Donald Trump, and others who are the best at what they do. They have studied, practiced, corrected their mistakes, learned from the past and others, and now are masters of their skill.

In this stage, a person has devoted hours and hours to hone in their skill. This is stage is not just for professional athletes. It can be for musicians, writers, carpenters, cabinet makers, police officers, stock investors, realtors, etc.

It takes thousands of hours of learning, practice, correction, and application for a person to master a skill. Once a person has mastered a skill, things come as second nature and actually feel like common sense to the person.

Stage One
Unconscious Incompetence

Most people in this stage have the desire to buy their first rental property but no knowledge of how, what, when, or where to buy a property. Even though they have the desire, they are unaware of what is possible with real estate investing (or any other industry), so typically their nature is skeptical.

Recently, I was on a phone call with a potential real estate coaching student who was very skeptical and pessimistic about real estate investing. He had seen many friends and family members by one or two properties, have a horrible experience and give up in frustration because they didn't know what they were doing.

This caused him to think that no one could ever make money from real estate investing. I could get offended, or take a step back and ask where this is really coming from. He was saying he was skeptical and also cynical because if this really were that easy, wouldn't everyone be doing it?

Every once in a while, I get asked this question, "If you are making so much money in real estate investing, why do you teach it?" Even though this is one of the most cynical questions you could ask, I don't get offended. I answer the question with another question.

"Who do you want to teach you how to invest in real estate? Someone who is not successful investing in real estate and who does NOT have a successful business?" This questions really drives home the point that you should only learn from those who are successful and are willing to give you their time to help you get to where they are.

Honestly, this is the reason why I coach others to invest in real estate. I am fully blessed to live the life of my dreams and I feel lead to give back to others the things that I have been blessed with. With my real estate investing, I could literally go fishing every day, binge watch Netflix or really, anything else? I don't need to do anything.

In fact, I make ridiculously more money investing in real estate than I do from anything else. It's not about the money. It is about helping others become successful. This is why I write books, have a podcast, write investing articles, and coach real estate investing.

I bring this up because you have to analyze where people like this are coming from. And they are just skeptical! They're cynical, and they doubt.

And they also have friends who don't believe as well as stoke that unbelief and skepticism. My desire is to take people from the stage of unconscious incompetence all the way to the conscious competence stage.

The people in this first stage are very skeptical though. They are skeptical because they do not have the knowledge of what is possible with investing in real estate. They don't know what they don't know. They are even stuck in their lack of knowledge AND do not want to get past this stage to better themselves.

There are many others who are stuck in this stage that could be holding you back from greatness. They do not want you to leave the group, to break away and try something different. When you do, it puts a spotlight on the fact that they are not doing something new.

There is a saying, "Misery loves company." They want you to stay with them because it validates their understanding, or lack thereof in real estate investing (or anything else). This is with anything in life. They are unaware and they doubt and try to make you second guess if this is something you really want to go after. These people are sometimes in your life as coworkers, friends, maybe even your spouse.

You have a choice when you encounter these nay-sayers. You need to ask yourself this question:

"Do I go back and do what I have always done, or push through and prove them wrong and prove to myself I can go in a different direction?"

If you are this person in this stage right now, I want you to ask yourself: Do I have a reason to be cynical, to doubt? Or should I be opening my mind and listening, perhaps someone else knows something I do not know?

Only you can make that decision if you are in this stage.

I will say that a lot of the time, when it is new and money is involved, it can be too good to be true. We have all been taught to think that way. This is a good perspective to have. You don't want to be swindled out of your hard-earned money. But, do not make the mistake of automatically shutting the door instead of investigating for yourself whether it is or not.

Real estate investing has been around ever since the beginning of time. People owned lands and properties since then and they will in the future. Rental properties have been around almost as long. People always will need a place to live and there will always be an investor like you who will be glad to accept their money to let them live in a property you own.

Stage Two
Conscious Incompetence

One student I was coaching started in this stage, as most do. My coaching student was young and very nervous about how he could actually quit his job by investing in real estate. He and his wife just had their first baby boy and he was exhausted from lack of sleep.

He knew it was possible to make money investing in real estate rental properties and had seen it done in the past by others. The thought of being able to provide for his family without working was a way that he could spend more time with his family. Without a J.O.B., he would be able to coach his son's little league games, be at home teaching his future children how to read and write, AND have the time to serve his church and his community.

He, like others in this stage, is aware that there is something they do not know but they are aware it is possible. Maybe a friend of theirs is starting to make money with rental property investing. People in this stage know that it is possible but you do not know how to start, let alone build a successful real estate rental business.

This is when you begin your search.

Maybe you listened to my podcast or saw my YouTube videos about investing in real estate. Maybe you start with something small, like learning how to get out of debt, because you have seen it been done and you now want to know how you can make money work for you.

Those in this stage are in a great position to take advantage of the great things that are out there. You are not just unaware, you are now aware of what is financially available to you, you just are incompetent to how it works. Again, this is a great place to be!

This means you are open to learning.

You've discovered that investing in real estate is possible and there are people like me who have mastered the game of passive income and want to share it with you. You are aware that people invest. Period. You just don't have the nuts and bolts to make it work for you. Yet.

I've been in this stage before, many times with many different subjects. It is as if there is SOOO much to learn and so little time. This is when your desire is to consume as much free content as you can! Yes! This is a great place to be.

This will get you started down the right path AND help you to know if this is really something you want to invest your time and money in. Take all the free content you can to learn!

Feel free to utilize all of my free content on my website: www.masterpassiveincome.com I want to see you succeed and this is the best way for you to get started. There are free articles, podcasts, tools, calculators, downloadable forms, etc. that will help you invest in real estate.

This stuff is not taught in schools and is NOT common sense. This is hard learned lessons of what is good, bad, and how to invest in real estate to change your life. This will also start to satisfy your curiosity. You will get familiar with the terms, ideas, and principles of real estate investing. BUT if you dive in to the deep in of the pool without learning how to swim, you may make some mistakes because at this level you are not an expert yet.

That is exactly what I did. I've lost tens of thousands of dollars doing real estate the wrong way. I did not continue to learn, get an online real estate investing course, or get coaching. I should have done all of these before, or even after I started investing. But I didn't.

Sometimes at this level, you could get caught up in: "I knew this wouldn't work" when you make an initial mistake. Even though it was tough. I didn't lose sight of the prize of a life without a J.O.B. I could have given up but I pushed through it.

But remember: You are still only at the free information! You are only at stage 2! It can be confusing with all of the ideas out there.

Be aware of negative voices, whether it's of others' or your own. And be aware that this is the level where you will make mistakes because you are determining different styles and different opinions. What's important at this step is to start learning and never stop.

For example, when I first started investing in real estate, I had the desire but not the knowledge. After taking a $1,000 2-day seminar on everything real estate investing, I decided to make a go for it. The seminar company was charging $30,000 for an "rental property course" that I could not afford, nor had the desire to spend that much money.

I knew I needed knowledge and training but knew that the most I would spend was $5,000 for coaching. Even though I didn't get into that coaching, looking back, it may have been a good investment. By doing it myself, I made so many mistakes which cost me loads of money.

Thinking of other ways to invest in real estate, I tried flipping properties. Even though this was good money, it did not allow me the freedom that I wanted to have. If I didn't flip a property, I wouldn't make any money. If I wasn't buying my next property, I would not have one to sell.

This is when I made the decision that lifestyle design and living the dream life was my goal. Not just another J.O.B.. After trying just about everything, I realized that rental property investing would be the only way that I could build wealth AND have a business that works without me.

The beauty of real estate investing is that it is an automatic business that runs itself. If I don't work, it still works for me.

For example, after I quit my job, I went on a 6-week trip

driving through Japan with my family. The year after, I took my family on another 6-week trip. This time it was through 11 counties in Europe. England, Scotland, Ireland, France, Germany, Switzerland, Israel, and many others.

This was all possible because of my rental property business. I work for 3 hours buying one property, then my business takes over and does all the work. This is how YOU can live the dream life! Build and automatic business that runs without you.

Truthfully, there is a right and wrong way to invest in real estate. When you are in this stage 2, focus on learning. Find someone who is already where you want to be. They have already done all the hard work. Now all you need to do is follow their lead.

Stage Three
Conscious Competence

At this level you are willing to try and are actively looking for solutions. You may have tried investing in real estate and may have had some success. You may have one, two, or three properties and are looking to become a serious real estate investor.

Now you are ready to be shown how to turn your one or two rental properties into a successful business. You look to someone else who has lived through this game for a while and now has the short cuts and tried and true strategies to learn from. They are able to help you build your business large enough to quit your J.O.B.

You do not have to make the same mistakes, that I made. You don't need to lose tens of thousands of dollars in your business to find the right way to do it. All you need to do is be given the direction to go, given a plan, be guided down the right roads, and save yourself all the headache.

This is the time for you to get coaching or find a mentor.

Someone who is already where you want to be AND show you how to get there.

Honestly, at this level, you are at the point where you are willing to pay for information. Not just information, but coaching and actual training.

It is no longer a matter of "Does this work?" for you. You are already there. You know it works. You have successes. You are ready for more.

It is a matter of: "How do I make it work BETTER and FASTER?"

At this level, impatience may kick in. It's working but maybe not as fast as you want. The problem with impatience is that you may move onto something else and then you start at the bottom of the ladder again at stage one.

If you start thinking, "Maybe I should learn something new – maybe now it's stocks". Now you are back to the free info, and you have to make your way all the way back to stage 3 (which is where you already were at!)

Every time you switch you typically go back to the bottom of the ladder.

Stage 3 is NOT about giving up or getting impatient when it doesn't work out like you thought. Typically, businesses see success after 5 years of business or thousands of hours to become an expert at a craft. This is where you need to hunker down and say "I am close!"

Seek out people and methods who are doing it BETTER and FASTER than you are at this stage and LEARN from them. Stick to your plan – do not let impatience draw you away from your game plan.

The healthy version is saying how do I make THIS work better and faster?

Stage Four
Unconscious Competence

This mastery can be applied to investing in real estate as it can to anything else.

This is the level of MASTERY. At this level, you have had success and are confident. This is where it becomes second nature to you.

Every month, I make tens of thousands of dollars in my real estate investing. This amount grows as I buy more and more properties. Remember, this is also without ANY work on my part. My business is an automatic business that runs without me.

Imagine making tens of thousands or even thousands of dollars each month without working...

Wouldn't your life change in amazing ways if you had an extra $1,000 a month in passive income? My first $1,000 in passive income was life changing for me. I was no longer Just Over Broke (J.O.B.). I had breathing room in my budget. The success bread more success.

Now, years later and 35 properties (currently), I have an automatic business that makes me tens of thousands of dollars a month. This is because I have mastered passive income.

Those in this stage are not as emotional as they once were in stage 1. You win some, you lose some. You have some evictions, and you have some big pay days. In the end, a real estate business is going to be NET positive at the end of the year.

The issue is most people do not allow enough time to let themselves get to this level. Some do not have the patience to attain it BUT we all want the RESULTS of the mastery level.

Most people want a 4-yr degree in the first year. That makes no sense. You would never go into college and say, "If I can't get this degree in year one this doesn't work and I want my money back."

If you flunk 1 or 2 classes you do NOT drop out and give up. You hire a tutor, you study and put more into it, and dissect the problem and how to get over it to get the degree.

Investing in real estate is no different: You need to move up all four stages to get really confident and gain the mastery level.

You cannot substitute time for this. You only become a master over time and from doing something over and over again. And most people don't stick with it and put in their thousands of hours so that they can get so good they don't need to think about it.

Where are YOU at in these stages?

Go back through all 4 stages... and see where you are currently at. If you are reading this book, you are either in, or very close to stage 2. If you want to progress to the next stage, there is only one thing you need to do.

Just get started learning.

For those who are at stage 3 and want to get serious about your real estate investing, consider joining a coaching program or get into an online course that will show you everything you need to build a successful business.

Or if you aspire to be at 4, you only get there by putting in the time and honing in your skill. Even at this level, you NEED to have a coach and community to stay accountable, to tell you when you need a course correction.

PHASE 2

Lay A Strong Foundation

PHASE 2.1
GET YOUR LIFE IN ORDER

"Today knowledge has power. It
controls access to opportunity and
advancement."

-Peter Drucker

I made a huge mistake.

This was not one of those mistakes that you can just shrug off and move past quickly. In the past, I had been able to muscle my way through anything. This time, I couldn't do that. It seemed as though this was one of those times when I just had to take my lumps.

When I first started investing in real estate, I just started buying properties. I did not stop to make sure I was buying the right properties, hiring the right property managers, and selecting the right tenants.

The decisions I was making were the best that I could have at the time. By learning through the school of hard knocks, I personally lost tens of thousands of dollars because I did not know what I was doing. When problems arose in the business, I would tell myself and my wife, "I'll figure it out..."

The problem was that in "Figuring it out" I was losing money. Lots of money.

- Over paying for properties.
- Missed inspections.
- Bad property manager stealing from me.
- Renting to bad tenants.
- Having to evict tenants after 2 months living in the property.
- Having evictions go against me for lack of following the laws.
- Paying way too much for repairs.
- Selling properties for a loss.
- If there was a bad decision to be made, I made it.

To be like the rich, you need to think like the rich and the rich continue to learn. They don't believe they know everything and can learn from anyone.

COMMIT TO SELF-EDUCATION

A seed planted will not grow unless it gets the nutrients it needs from the soil around it and the correct amount of water. If the seed is sewn on rocky ground where there is not much soil, the seed may get water, but it will not get the nutrients it needs because there is little soil.

If the seed is sown on a path, it will get eaten by the birds and never have a chance to start the growing process. The only way for a plant to grow is to be properly planted where it can get the nutrients it needs for it to grow, then God does the rest of the work.

Likewise, the only way for you to grow is to get the nutrients you need in order for you to grow. By educating yourself like the rich, you will gain the knowledge, wisdom, and examples you need to grow into the person you want to be. If you want to learn how to be a piano player, do you educate yourself on how to be a plumber? No, that would be crazy.

To be like the rich, you need to learn from the rich. Try to find those around you who are where you want to be, and learn as much as you can from them. Find a mentor/coach, listen to podcasts, read books, etc. If you educate yourself about how to be like the rich, you will be able to design your life the way you want it and be free from having to work a job your entire life.

There is a saying that I want you to remember:

"A smart man learns from his mistakes. A wise man learns from others mistakes."

Be wise and learn from others mistakes. Learn from my mistakes. I have made just about every mistake you possibly could in this business. Even though I've made mistakes, I've learned from them and applied those lessons into my business.

You can do bypass all the problems, loss of money, and heartache by following the way that I invest and implement them into your business. Like many others have done, I will show you how you can quit your J.O.B. with rental property investing.

PRINCIPLES OF THE RICH

There is a reason why the majority of the people in the world are poor. It is because they are not taught to be rich. They don't know the principles that the rich already know and implement in their lives. If you knew the principles of the rich, you could change your life and be rich as well.

I want you to be rich. Scratch that. Not just rich, but wealthy. The principles of the rich apply to everyone, today, tomorrow, and far into the future. No matter if you read this 20 years from now or 200 years from now, these principles will still help you become wealthy and rich.

There was a time when I was spending the money my properties were bringing in and I was not able to continue buying properties because I spent all the rent money. This set me back six months and I eventually relearned one of the key lessons of the book.

With the help of these principles, I have been able to build a real estate empire, create massive amounts of wealth, and master passive income. I'm going to share with you these principles as I have learned them and how you can make them a part of your life. If you apply these rules to your life and financial understanding, you too can become rich too.

THIS MONEY IS TO BE SAVED, AND NOT SPENT, FOR FUTURE INVESTING. AFTER TIME, YOUR BANK ACCOUNT BALANCE BEGINS TO GROW BIGGER AND BIGGER.

Principle 1: Pay Yourself First

The first principle of the rich is probably the simplest to do, but the hardest to implement. To start growing your wealth, you must pay yourself first. This sounds a little counter intuitive because when you get your paycheck from your job, you actually receive your money from your employer and it's yours. In reality, your paycheck has already been spent.

Reoccurring monthly expenses take your money every month so it is not actually your money. We all have monthly expenses that take our money. Things like a home mortgage or rent, car payments, health insurance, electricity, food, and every other luxury and necessity in life. These items own your money, while you own nothing.

To pay yourself first it means for every $100 that you take home, you keep in your savings or bank account 10% or $10. This money is to be saved, and not spent, for future investing. After time, your bank account balance will begin to grow bigger and bigger.

Over time you will have much more money in your bank account then when you did when you started. Be careful not to spend this money on anything that will not make you more money. New cars, big tv's, vacations, etc. are all types of items that take money out of your account but do not put any back.

You can start this first principle right away with your next paycheck you receive by taking out 10% and save it for a future investment of a rental property. If your paycheck is $1,000 then pay yourself $100 and save it. The rest of the nine hundred dollars will then go to pay your bills and other expenses you have, but that one hundred dollars is yours to keep.

If you get paid every other week, you would get paid 26 times a year and saving $100 times 26 pay periods equals $2,600 saved up over the year! Not to mention the interest you would gain if you put it in a bank account that earns interest. Over time, you would have enough saved for a down payment on a home for yourself. You would be able to stop renting and move into a home that you own.

You now own a piece of property that you can rent out in the future when you move into another house you buy with your savings!

Principle 2: Increase Your Income

The second principle of the rich is to find ways to increase your income. When we were young, we went to school to learn different subjects. When we are older, we choose which subjects we want to learn. The poor do not continue to educate themselves but rather work a job and stay the same place their entire life.

Self-education and continuing education are the key to success in life and wealth for your future.

As you educate yourself more, become wiser and more skillful, you will be able to reach higher heights and go beyond your natural limit. When you do start to increase your abilities, you should put them to good work. You do this by applying your skills in a way that helps you to earn more money so that you can invest in your future.

I am constantly learning from anyone and everyone I meet. I strive to be better than I currently am. To be a constant learner, you should be able to learn from anyone. Be it the CEO of a major corporation, to a grocery store clerk, or anyone else, you can always learn something new.

It is all in the mentality of being teachable and not let your pride stop you from learning. The more you learn the more you will be able to harness your abilities to find new ways to make more money. In doing this, you will make your life more fulfilling.

There is something to watch out for when you start to increase your earning potential. The tempting thing to do is to increase your standard of living when your income rises. The mentality of a poor person is to immediately spend any money they receive when they get a raise from their boss. Buying a new car, buying a bigger house, buying the luxuries that they desire are all things that will take away your ability to buy more investments that make you money and lasting wealth.

They do not think like the rich. The rich mentality is to use the increase in income to purchase more investments that bring them in more money. The rich don't deprive themselves of what they desire, instead they purchase investments that buy them what they desire.

Famous investor and writer Robert Kiyosaki wanted a new Porsche to drive. He had done very well with investments and saved up $300,000 to buy a new Porsche. Robert understands how to think like the rich, do you think he paid cash for it? No, he didn't. Since Robert uses the principles of the rich to become even richer, he took out a loan for the Porsche even though he had the ability to buy it with cash.

Many of you may be saying; "What, why would he want to pay all the interest on the $300,000 car?" Instead of buying the $300,000 Porsche in cash, he made the decision to buy an investment that would make enough money to afford the monthly payments. After he bought the investment property, he had $3000 a month to afford the payments on a $300,000 car.

Taking the $300,000, Robert instead bought an apartment complex and invested his money. Now, that $300,000 is working for him, making him money. Each month, he receives the rent payment and uses the passive income from the apartment to pay the car loan. There are three things that really stand out with using the principles of the rich in this way.

1. The tenants pay Robert rent which pays for the apartment expenses AND the loan payment for the Porsche.

2. After the Porsche is paid off, buy the tenants, he no longer owes the bank for the car loan AND still owns the income

producing apartment complex.

3. He can use the money from the car loan payment to buy a new Porsche once he is tired of that one.

This must be stated again to drive home this point. The beauty of using your money to work for you in this way is that after the Porsche is paid for by his tenants, Robert still has the investment of the apartment complex. Once the Porsche is paid off, his investment is still bringing in enough money to buy another Porsche if he wanted to. On top of that, his original $300,000 is protected and saved in the apartment complex.

This is how the rich think. They buy investments that help them to buy other the items that they desire.

Principle 3: Control Your Expenses

The third principle of the rich is to control your expenses. This principle teaches us to live below our means and not over spend. The key to this goes with the first principle. Make sure you don't spend more than 90% of your earnings because the last 10% is to pay yourself first. The only real way to do this is to list out exactly what your expenses are each month, then cut out expenses to get you below 90% of your income.

In order to have more money in your pocket that you can save for investing, you need to either increase income or decrease expenses. Cutting expenses is hard to do but must be done in order for you to be rich.

As in the previous example of $1,000 per paycheck, if your expenses are $1,000 per pay period, you are not making any money but are just living paycheck to paycheck which most Americans do. Your goal should be to cut out expenses so you have more money to save for future investments.

Current Monthly Expenses	Possible Monthly Expenses
Rent Large House - $1,600	Rent Medium House - $1,100
Rent Large House - $1,600	Rent Medium House - $1,100
Verizon Cell Phone - $75	Go Phone $40
Cable Television - $100	Free Over the Air TV + Hulu and Netflix - $16
Car Payment - $300 - $15,000 Value	Sell the car for $15,000 and buy a $3,000 beater - $0
Eating Out - $600	Make meals at home - $200
Entertainment - $250	Red box movie rentals - $15
Gym Membership - $50	Work out at home - $0
Total Monthly Expense - $2,975	Total Monthly Expense - $1,371
	Savings of $1,604 Monthly!

Take time today to list out monthly expenses and get very detailed. Once you have a list of all the items you spend your money on, go through the list and figure what you can actually cut from your life to save more money for investment. I suggest cutting out as many expenses you can, almost to where it may actually start to hurt.

Do you really need the NFL package with your television? Do you have time to watch all 500 channels you pay for each month? Maybe drop the plan to only have 60 channels and save $50 a month.

Or what about your cell phone bill, do you really need 15 to 20 gigabytes of data or can you stop the data plan and just find Wi-Fi locations to use the internet? Doing this exercise will lower your expenses and save you money.

Principle 4: Buy the Home You Live In

This principle is about buying your home and not renting it. When you are a renter, you are giving your money away to someone else. The home you are renting right now may cost you $1,200 a month in rent. The landlord of the property is not in business to lose money so he is probably making money each month from the rent you pay.

If his expenses are $900 a month, and your rent is $1,200, you are giving him $300 dollars of your income for the "privilege" of living in his home. That is another $300 that could be in your pocket every month, or $3,600 per year! Find a home you can afford, while keeping the 10% to pay yourself first, purchase it and cut your expenses that you would normally have in renting a property.

Principle 5: Insure A Future Income

This principle is to protect yourself and your investments with insurance. Insuring your properties that you own against loss and liability is a must. You do not live in the rental property but you allow others to do so. Insurance protects yourself from damages to the property the tenant causes and even liability issues from the tenant.

If someone slips and falls on your property, you are potentially liable to be sued for damages. Make sure that you have liability coverage over the property to protect yourself from being sued in the future. Insurance is relatively low in cost and will save you if you ever need it.

If you have any family at all, personal life insurance is also a very good way to take care of them in the event of your passing. I know that my wife and kids are taken care of in the event of my passing because of the life insurance that I have myself. My wife will be able to pay off the house and live just fine for the rest of her life because of the insurance and rental properties that we own.

Principle 6: Make Your Money Work for You

The sixth principle of the rich is to make your money work for you. After you have started saving 10% of your income and cut out your expenses until it hurts, then you are ready to look at what to do with your money.

This is the point where you can spend your money on investments that earn you more money. There are 6 ways rental properties make you money and we will go over those in the next chapter.

It is said that the majority of the wealthy rich people in the world hold their money in real estate and the reason why is you do not lose your money in fact you actually gain money through depreciation, cash flow, and tax benefits.

An example of what you should buy with your savings is a rental property that brings in $300 a month into your pocket. An example of what you don't want to buy is a flashy new car that does not bring money into your pocket but takes money out of it.

Principle 7: Guard Yourself from Losing Money

The seventh principle of the rich is to not lose money. After you have worked hard to save 10%, cut your expenses until it hurts, and then look for an opportunity for your money work for you. When you invest your money in rental properties, you have placed it in a safe investment for the future.

When you are looking for an investment for your money, there are two things to keep in mind: Risk and Return. The goal is to find the investment that has the lowest risk with the highest return. Everyone knows that stocks, mutual funds, IRA's, and 401k's are types of investments because you are investing in businesses.

I prefer to invest in a business I can control and the real estate rental properties that my company owns are completely under my control. The main reasons why I invest in rental properties have the lowest risk and highest return of all other investments.

Here is an example of the types of returns you can see with a single-family rental property.

Single Family Property	
Purchase Price: $100,000	
Down Payment: $20,000 Closing Costs: $2,500 Carrying Costs until rented: $800 Rehab costs: $12,000 Mortgage Payments: $4,800 First year maintenance: $600	Monthly Rent Amount: $900
First Year Expenses: $ 49,700	Total First Year Rent: $10,800
Cash on Cash Return: $10,800 / $49,700 = 22%	Yearly Return for year one: 22%

It would be very unlikely to get a rate of return of 22% in a mutual fund but 22% is actually a low number for rental properties. Imagine if you put no money down, which is possible, to buy a rental property and have the same monthly rent. Your rate of return could not be calculated because it would be infinite since you had no money out of your pocket.

Another thing to watch out for is buying useless things with the money you make from your investment. If you buy a piece of real estate that brings in $300 a month and you go and spend $300 a month on something like a new car, you are hindering the growth of your wealth. That money should be saved for future investing.

Think of each of your dollars as little employees working hard for you day and night for you to make more money. The beautiful thing is that you are now able to take your profits from the rental property to buy more investments. With those investments, you are able to make even more money which allows you to buy more investments that makes you even more money.

If you save the $300 a month from your rental, you will have $3,600 each year to save on top of your 10% you are already saving from your income!

Principle 8: It Is Better to Give Than Receive

This last principle of the rich is that it is better to give than receive. I have always been taught that is better to give than receive, and I have found that be true. This lesson seems counter intuitive but the more money I give, the more money I receive.

I don't necessarily receive the money from the person that I gave it to, but it comes back to me in other ways. I find that the more honest I am with my money and the more that I use my money to help other people the more I get in return.

The money that we are given from God belongs to Him. We are just stewards of His money and His possessions. We are just blessed to be stewards of it. He allows us to keep 90% of his money that we receive and give back to him only 10%. I have found that the more I give, the more I receive in return from God.

God doesn't need the 10% that we give back to him, because he owns it all, but in reality, giving the 10% is for us. It is for us to not let money control us or who we are. The great thing though is that the more I give, the less money has a hold of me, and the more I rely on God for my every need.

These principles the rich live by will change your life if you implement them into your daily living. I encourage you to implement these into your financial mindset. Move yourself from thinking as the poor do and start to think as the rich do.

I have implemented them in my life which has helped me to get to where I am today. These principles are not rocket science, they are however hard to follow though. This is because of the many years of living life without the knowledge and experience, and not applying these principles to assist us in our life. If you start today and apply these to your life, you will see many changes in you that will help you in your future.

IDENTIFY YOUR CURRENT FINANCIAL SITUATION

"What a banker WILL ask for is your financial statement. Your financial statement is your report card for the real world."

– Robert Kiyosaki

Everyone has a starting point on any journey they take. Because of life experiences, some may be further along or behind than others. In order to take the first step, you need to assess where you are on the journey. Once you find your starting point, you will be able to know how to take that first step on the journey to becoming rich.

Every investor must start at this same step, and that is knowing your finances. The first step in the long journey is to find out your current financial situation with the attached financial worksheet. This can be a difficult process to go through, but it is crucial because all the other steps build off of this.

When I started, I had to go through the same process of discovery and transformation in my finances. I hated not knowing what happened to my money at the end of the month because I didn't plan or manage my money well. I am blessed to have a terrific wife who is great with numbers to help get our financial house in order.

It is tempting but DON'T skip this step.

Your financial worksheet is the foundation you have been building built your entire life, and it is time find out how solid that foundation is. Take the time right now and complete the financial worksheet on the next page.

CREATE A PLAN AND A BUDGET TO SAVE FOR FUTURE INVESTING

"We must consult our means rather than our wishes."

– George Washington

Creating and sticking to a budget for you and your family is an extremely important practice that you must implement into your life. Without a budget, you will wonder where your money went at the end of the month. You don't want to be in a place where there is more month left at the end of the money.

By creating a budget, you tell your dollars what they are to be used for AND you are able to plan how much you can save for future investing. They say that cash is king, and in the investing world, it is even truer than ever.

When you are creating your budget, be specific and be accurate. The more accurate you are with the numbers, the more likely you will be able to stay on budget and begin saving money for future investing.

Also, you may find that you may be over spending in some areas and are possibly going into debt by your spending. Cut out wasted spending with a passion. Your goal should be to save 10% of your income for future investing.

Quick Budget Worksheet & Financial Statement

As you have already seen, I have a free worksheet for you to download. In it, there is a "Quick Budget" guide and a "Financial Worksheet" that will help you get your finances in order. Fill out both of these sheets so you can see where you are financially and make changes to help you increase your ability to invest in the future.

Download all the free goodies here:
http://www.masterpassiveincome.com/free-action-guide

Taking Action for Phase 2.1

➢ Download and complete Financial Statement. Make sure you account for everything and fill out the statement fully. This will be what you will use to help bankers know you are a person they will want to lend money to in the future.

➢ Download and complete the Quick Budget Worksheet. Fill it out completely and leave nothing out. Use your bank statement, credit card statement, and other spending trackers to make sure you account for all of your money spent in one month.

➢ Analyze your budget. Where are you spending money that you shouldn't? Where can money be better spent?

➢ Analyze your debt. Do you have consumer debt? i.e. credit cards, car payments, etc. Aggressively attack that consumer debt by doing a debt snowball.

  o Debt snowball: pay as much as you can toward the account that has the smallest balance to get rid of that debt. Once that is paid off, move that entire payment over to the next credit card that has the lowest amount. Once that is paid off, do it again to the next lowest. Keep going until all the debt is paid off.

PHASE 2.2

WHY YOU SHOULD INVEST IN RENTAL PROPERTIES

The adrenaline pumped through my veins.

Looking at the flickering neon Coca Cola sign in the retail business I started 6 months prior, I envisioned my not-so-distant future ahead of me. A future where I would never have to work for anyone ever again. I had just gotten back from an on-site visit to Youngstown Ohio where I had recently put in an offer for an investment home for $17,000 in cash.

"Okay Dustin, the property is yours," Dave, my seasoned Realtor informed me over the phone from Ohio. Even though I was living in California, I saw the potential of real estate in other areas of the country and bought another rental property there. My goal was not to flip houses, but to own and rent them.

"Terrific, thanks Dave! Please give the keys to my property manager so she can get the place rented." I replied with a little anxiety in my voice. It took a lot of convincing for my wife to agree to spend our life savings on an investment property 3000 miles away.

My sales pitch to her was that we would earn passive income in monthly cash flow by renting the house to tenants we would never meet.

Since this was the first investment property we had ever bought, it was quite the nerve-racking experience, filled with uncertainty and doubt.

The following questions came to my mind:
- ➢ Did I do the right thing with our life savings?
- ➢ Was this the right house to buy for an investment?
- ➢ Was this the right area to invest in?
- ➢ What if the house caught fire and burnt down?
- ➢ What would we do if we get horrible tenants?
- ➢ What will we do if the furnace goes out and there is a $2500 expense?
- ➢ How do we manage a rental property when we have never done it before?

After hanging up the phone with my realtor, all these questions and more swirled inside my head. For some reason, though, maybe it is the optimist in me, I knew everything would be just fine. Looking back now, everything has been just fine, as long as we kept the course of building businesses with passive income.

For the next nine years, every penny I earned from the passive income went back into the business to make more passive income. Year after year, I bought more and more properties. Each property brought in more money that I would then use to buy more properties.

SIX WAYS RENTAL PROPERTIES MAKE YOU MONEY

The average rate of return for the stock market is at best at 10% return every year. A 30% return on your money in rental properties seems like it would be extremely high compared to the 10% from the stock market. Actually, a 30% return in real estate is very low and I may even pass on a deal with only 30% return. I have seen returns as much as 100%, 200%, and even 500% with my rental properties.

If you invest in the stock market, you only get one way you make money. Appreciation of the stock. As the value of the stock goes up, so does the money you make. Buy low and sell high is what stock traders do. If they buy the stock at $100 and sell it at $150, then they made $50 or 50% return on their money. But this is hard to do. Stocks don't move that fast.

In real estate though, there are six ways that you make money when you buy them as rental properties and hold onto them for years. Other investments have one or two of these ways but rental properties have all of them.

1. Cash flow from monthly rent

When you buy your rental properties, you must buy them in such a way that you earn cash flow from day one. The rent minus expenses is your cash flow for the property. It is not uncommon to have anywhere from $200-$300 in monthly cash flow from each property you own.

It is as easy as doing math you learned in elementary school. If you buy a rental property that has a monthly rent amount of $1,100, and the total expenses are $800, you profit $300 each month the properties rented.

2. Equity Capture

You MAKE your money on a real estate purchase when you BUY the house. You REALIZE the money when you SELL it. Buy low, sell high. Just as you buy the property to earn cash flow from day one, you also want to buy the property below market value, so you automatically gain equity on the property. If a three-bedroom, two bath, single family home market value is $120,000 and you buy it for $100,000, you automatically gain $20,000 in equity for the property.

You, as an investor, want to get paid for the value that you bring, not the hours that you work. To build up equity yourself, you can find the worst house in the best neighborhood, fix it up with minor repairs like paint, carpet, etc., and make the value of the home increase beyond the current market value.

> YOU MAKE YOUR MONEY ON A REAL ESTATE PURCHASE WHEN YOU BUY THE HOUSE. YOU REALIZE THE MONEY WHEN YOU SELL IT.

The same $120,000 home that you bought for $100,000 will be worth $140,000 after you fix up the property and make it worth more. Also, when you build the value, the rental income goes up because the property demands a higher rent due to the superior property compared to the others for rent in the area.

3. Forced Appreciation

As investors, we do not want to buy the best and prettiest house on the street. It is best to buy properties that you can put some work into to make the value of the property to go up. This would not necessarily be a major remodel like tearing down half the house to rebuild it. These would be cosmetic things that would make the property look clean and nice.

Here are some things to look for:

1. Exterior and interior paint needed
2. Front yard landscaping
3. New carpet or flooring
4. New fixtures for lighting and plumbing
5. New baseboards and trim.

These are relatively inexpensive repairs that you can do to make the value of the property go up.

It is not uncommon to spend $10,000 fixing up the property and force the appreciation up by $25,000 to $30,000.

4. Market appreciation

For the last 200 years, the real estate market has doubled in value every 20 years. Two of the main reasons for this are inflation and interest rates. The value of the dollar is reflected in the current gold price. An ounce of gold is worth the same 200 years ago as it is now.

It is just the way in which we buy the gold that has changed in value. The dollar, through inflation, has lost its buying power over the years because of inflation. More recently quantitative easing (governments' term for printing money out of thin air with nothing backing the value of it) was implemented in order to attempt to stimulate the economy.

With inflation, the homes you buy will increase in dollar value and history shows the value doubles every 20 years. Interest rates are also a cause for price fluctuations in the real estate market. As interest rates lower, which we have seen in the past 10 years, prices go up because the ability to borrow money is cheap (currently 3%-4% interest rate), and people can buy more expensive homes for less money each month out of their pocket.

If people can only afford a $1,500 a month mortgage

payment, a $400,000 home at 4% interest for 30 years is a home they can afford. But if the interest is at 9% (as it was in the '80s and '90s) for 30 years, their $1,500 a month will only allow them to buy a $235,000 home.

5. Equity Buildup

As rents pay down the mortgage balance, the equity increase is considered profit. The equity is only on paper until you sell or refinance the property.

I have personally used the equity in all my properties many, many times. Each time I have enough equity in the property to pull out $50,000 or more, I did. This is the best form of using "O.P.M." or Other People's Money.

Each time I refinance and take money out of a property to buy another property, I am just recycling my money over and over again. Each time I do, I make even more money each month in passive income. You will learn more about it in the Rental Property 2.0 chapter.

6. Tax Deductions

Write-Off Business Expenses

All your business expense you incur in your business, you can use that to offset how much of your income is taxed. Here is a small list of a few items you can write-off:

- Cell phone
- Mileage traveled
- Home office
- Electronics used for your business
- Home internet
- Property taxes
- Professional fees (accountants, lawyers, etc.)

- Taxes
- Business Education
- Conventions
- Seminars

Take your time and really analyze all of the expenses for your business. Since Real Estate is a business, your operating expenses can be deducted from your income. Mortgage interest, insurance, repairs, advertising, Property Manager, utilities, yard maintenance, losses, etc., are all items that can be deducted from your income which lowers your income liability.

Depreciation

The IRS lets you deduct the value of the property over 27.5 years. Depreciation is looked at as an expense, but no money was ever spent. You purchased the property, which makes you money and still has its actual value, and the IRS lets you deduct part of the value of the property over 27.5 years.

Another great thing about depreciation is that if you give the property to your children, they get to start the entire depreciation cycle of 27.5 years all over again at the current market value!

1031 Exchange

How much of the tax advantage you will get from depreciation depends on your tax bracket and your sources of income. It's generally around 5 to 15% ROI from this tax advantage on your initial investment.

No other asset class can match with real estate rental properties. Stocks, bonds, money market accounts, etc. are all good investments but pale in comparison to real estate. With real estate, you build real wealth that is tangible. You can pass it down to your children, grandchildren, and anyone else you want to bless with wealth. With these six-ways you make money in real estate, it is very hard to lose in real estate investing.

THREE WAYS TO INCREASE EQUITY

There are three ways you can create equity with rental properties. Each of these are built into the system of buying right, renting the property, and getting paid for the value that you bring, not the hours that you work.

1. Reduce Debt

With the monthly rent you collect each month, part of the money goes to pay the mortgage you took for the purchase of the property. A $100,000 home, which can be rented for $1,200 per month, with a 4%, 30-year mortgage is only $477 per month. That leaves $723 per month to pay the property manager and the expenses. The balance is yours to keep as passive income.

This must point cannot be over-stated. You are not personally paying the principle balance of the loan, nor are you paying the interest on the principle. Your tenant is the one paying for the home.

> YOU ARE NOT PERSONALLY PAYING THE PRINCIPLE BALANCE OF THE LOAN, NOR ARE YOU PAYING THE INTEREST ON THE PRINCIPLE. YOUR TENANT IS THE ONE PAYING FOR THE HOME.

Really consider this. If you buy a home with an FHA Loan (Federal Housing Administration), you would put 3.5% down on a rental property. If it were a $100,000 property, that would be $3,500 down payment. The balance owed on the property is $96,500 plus the interest that is incurred with the loan.

Even though the loan is in your name, you are not paying it yourself. You don't need to get another job to pay the mortgage.

Your new property is working for you. It is a part of your inventory that is making you money month after month AND paying for itself.

2. Make Money on the First Day You Own the Property

You make money when you buy your rental properties because, like stocks, you buy low and sell high. Your goal is to never lose money and you can only do that if you buy a house that fits our criteria that it will make you money when you buy it.

Let's say you find a deal on a property that is worth $150,000, but you can buy it for $100,000. That is an instant $50,000 equity that is kept in your investment. When you want to cash out the $50,000, you can either refinance the property and get a note for the equity, or sell the property and pocket the difference. Remember, you make money when you BUY the property, not when you sell it.

3. Forced Appreciation Through Rehab

You can increase the value of the same property you just bought for $100,000 by rehabbing it. You can remodel the kitchen and bathrooms, add fresh paint, install new flooring, fix up the front and backyard, add another room, etc.

The property that had a market value of $150,000 may now be worth $200,000 even though you only spent $20,000 to fix up the property. Basically, you can make the property more attractive to future buyers by fixing it up, and that makes the value of the property increase.

NON-MONETARY REASONS TO OWN RENTAL PROPERTIES

There are many non-monetary reasons why rental properties are amazing investments. Here are 11 other reasons real estate rental properties are the best investment:

Complete Control Over Your Investments

Unlike stocks, where you have no control over the business, you have complete control over your real estate business. Want to increase rents? Increase the value of the property. Need to replace an AC unit and want to save money by buying a smaller unit because the original was too big?

That is your choice.

Want to pass on a tenant that has bad credit and prior evictions? Again, these are all in your control. You have complete control over the business and property to do as you see fit.

Owning Real Estate is Seen as a Business

Because owning rental properties is seen by the IRS as a business, you get many tax deductions. These deductions make it look like your passive income is lower and because of that, you save money.

Depreciation

The IRS lets you deduct the value of the property over 27.5 years. Depreciation is looked at as an expense, but no money was ever spent. You purchased the property, which makes you money and still has its actual value, and the IRS lets you deduct part of the value of the property over 27.5 years.

Another great thing about depreciation is that if you give the property to your children, they get to start the entire depreciation cycle of 27.5 years all over again at the current market value!

Operating expenses

Mortgage interest, insurance, repairs, advertising, Property Manager, utilities, yard maintenance, losses, etc.

Ownership expenses

Property taxes, mileage, business cell phone, professional fees for accountants and lawyers, travel, convention attendance, business education, home office, etc.

Taxes on Your Properties Can Be Deferred Almost Indefinitely

With real estate, you can defer the taxes you incur when you sell your property almost indefinitely. With an IRS 1031 exchange, you can exchange the property for a like-kind investment. Like-kind is real estate exchanged for more valuable real estate.

Like-kind is not selling a coffee shop business in exchange for real estate. For example, you buy a single-family home, sell it 10 years later, and make $50,000.

You can use a 1031 exchange to buy a more expensive property like another single-family home that makes more income or even an apartment building! Do all this without paying any taxes today and defer them to a much later date if you decide to cash out completely.

No Liability, But All the Control

When you purchase properties as rentals, the best way to own the property is with a company like an LLC. You want to "control" the rental properties and not "own" them. You may buy your personal residence in your name, but the investment properties should be put into a company you create, like an LLC or an S-Corp.

An LLC is a Limited Liability Company that you own and control, and the LLC then owns the property. Since it is the LLC that owns the property and not you personally, if the property ever gets sued, you are not personally liable and your assets will be safe. Remember that you "control" the property, not own it.

Low Volatility in the Real Estate Market

Unlike the stock market, the real estate market does not change overnight. Even if the real estate market crashes, as it did in 2007, you are able to see it coming as well as get out of the way if needed.

But no matter what happens in the market, if you learn how to buy right, you will never have to worry about another crash in the real estate market because your rent still comes in every month.

Making Money In An Up or Down Market

Even better, though, is if you purchase your properties right and they cash flow from day one, you will not have to worry about an up or down market. Since the mortgage is fixed at 30 years, and you have income coming in to cover the expenses, you will always make money.

Rarely do rents ever go down, and actually they are always going up with inflation. In an up market, you can sell your properties and use a 1031 exchange and buy a better property with your gains. Also, in a down market, homes are cheaper, and the rent to purchase price is more in your favor.

Constant Demand for your Product

The product you are selling is basically a place to live for anyone. No matter what happens to the economy, people need a place to live and will be there to sign a lease with you for the property that you own. Since everyone needs a place to live, your product will never go out of style.

Use O.P.M. to Start Your Real Estate Rental Business with Leverage

Go ahead and ask a banker to lend you $100,000 to buy stock in Apple or Microsoft. He would laugh you out of his office. Now ask the same banker to lend the same $100,000 to you to buy a home; be ready to sign the contract.

Leverage is the most widely used means to acquire rental properties because banks are so willing to lend to the right investor who knows how to manage properties.

Leveraging a property and taking on a mortgage is using other people's money to make you money. When you buy a home with all cash, your rate of return (return of money that you put into the deal) is much lower than if you use leverage.

Purchase an $80,000 home:

Paying cash in the amount of $80,000 would bring you $8,400 a year income. This consists of equity capture of $18,000, appreciation of $5,000 and cash flow of $8,400 with a total return of 38% on the $80,000 you spent.

You use leverage and put a down payment of $8,000 for the $80,000 home which brings you $2,400 a year in income. This consists of equity capture of $16,000, equity increase from mortgage payments of $600, appreciation of $5,000 and cash flow of $2,400, which is a total return of 200% on the $8,000 you spent.

Hedge Against Inflation

Inflation averages about 3% per year. If you keep your money in the bank earning .01% per year in your savings account, you are losing money every day. You may be gaining a few meager dollars, but those dollars buy less and less every year.

As you can see from the savings vs. inflation image to the right, your $10,000 you saved for ten years with simple interest makes you $10 in interest. After the same ten years, your original $10,000 can only buy $9,930 worth of goods.

So, you may gain $10 after ten years but you lose $30 because of inflation which makes a net loss of $20.04 after ten years. In the Savings vs. Inflation chart, you can see that the buying power lessens as time goes on because of inflation.

Savings vs. Inflation

.01% APR Savings		3% Inflation Per Year	
Year	Balance	Year	Buying Power
1	$10,001.00	1	$9,997.00
2	$10,002.00	2	$9,994.00
3	$10,003.00	3	$9,991.00
4	$10,004.00	4	$9,987.99
5	$10,005.00	5	$9,984.99
6	$10,006.00	6	$9,981.98
7	$10,007.00	7	$9,978.98
8	$10,008.00	8	$9,975.97
9	$10,009.00	9	$9,972.96
10	$10,010.00	10	$9,969.96

Insure Your Investment

You can insure your rental properties against things like loss, theft, fire, and liability. Just like you cannot get a loan for stocks, ask insurance brokers to give you insurance for losses in the stock market. They would laugh at you and then kick you out of the office.

If you own a rental property with a replacement value of $250,000, you can pay yearly insurance on the property of only $700 for full coverage and protect your investment. How could that get any better? Easy!

Have your tenants pay for the insurance by adding it into your numbers when you purchase the property. $700 a year is $58.33 a month. When you run the numbers when you purchase a property, make sure the costs of insurance are in there so you have it covered by the rents the tenants pay.

CREATE YOUR GOALS FOR FUTURE SUCCESS

"All our dreams can come true if we have the courage to pursue them."

– Walt Disney

"10 years…" I said one day out of the blue to my brother Sky.

"What in the world are you talking about?" he asked.

"I'm tired man. Aren't you?" I replied.

"You tired? Your only 27 years old… What do you have to be tired about?"

"Actually, I'm tired of having a J.O.B. and I'm tired of being just-over-broke. My J.O.B. is holding me back. 40+ hours a week of my life being wasted for nothing. Being told what to do by a horrible boss, and having to put up with absolutely ridiculous co-workers…" I said.

"Well, what does that have to do with 10 years?" he asked.

"You know the definition of insanity is doing the same thing over and over again expecting a different result. Well, it's time to make a change. I'm giving myself 10 more years of drudging through this J.O.B. and then I'm quitting" I said.

"Wow, what will you do to pay your bills? What will you do to provide for your family? What will you do to make sure you do not have to go back to that J.O.B.?" he asked.

"Two words... Passive income" I said.

"I've heard of it. But we've been taught our entire lives to be employees. It is never taught in school how to make passive income. How will you learn how to do it and how will you make sure it works" he asked?

"Two more words for you... Rental properties..." I replied.

"Awesome! That is a great goal and rental properties are a fantastic stream of income for anyone. You know what, I'm in..." Sky stated.

"What?! You're in?!" I asked.

"Yep, I'm in. That will be my goal too. 10 years to create businesses, buy investments, and create enough passive income to quit my J.O.B." he exclaimed.

"Alright bro! Let's do it! Actually, it's a race. Let's work together and have a friendly competition to see who can do it first. But, after 10 years, we must quit our J.O.B." I said enthusiastically.

"Done... and Done..." he said.

I tell you this story because this was what got me determined to make my dream come true. Working a J.O.B. would never allow me to live the dream life so I needed a change and a challenge. With us working together and encouraging each other, we beat our goal of 10 years.

Truth be told, Sky beat me to the goal. He actually beat me because he got laid off at year 7. At the time, it was rough because he was not 100% ready and this would have been a bad situation if he had not been building up his business. BUT, because he had his passive income businesses, he was not even worried. Now, it has been 5 years since he was laid off and he will NEVER work a job again.

I was able to quit my job at year 6 but was very nervous to do so. Giving up that steady paycheck is a hard thing to do. By the end of year 8, I couldn't quit fast enough... I quit at the beginning of year 9 and will NEVER work a J.O.B. again!

HOW TO SET YOUR GOALS TO QUIT YOU J.O.B.

In America, about 3% of the population set goals for themselves. Just by making goals for yourself, you already have a head start to becoming rich. 67% of rich people set goals for themselves in life and business as opposed to 8% of the poor.

By setting goals for yourself and writing them down, you are creating a roadmap to your life. Think of where you want to be in five years and start with that end in mind. Below is your primer to get yourself on the path of goal setting.

When I was 27 years old, I told my wife of 3 months that I was going to quit my job. Not having a job of her own, she was concerned. When I told her it would be in 10 years, she was a little relieved but was still worried about how we were going to make money. Because I set goals for myself, I had something to aim for to keep me motivated and pushing for the goal of quitting my J.O.B.

71

Have A Vision for the Future You Want for Yourself

Picture how you want your life to be in five years. That is called having a vision and being able to see what has not come to be. A vision for your life is a picture or an idea of where you want to be if you could design your life the way you want it. If you are able to create a master vision for your life, that vision is basically a destination you can strive towards.

WHEN YOU ARE SETTING YOUR FIVE-YEAR GOALS, TRY USE YOUR VISION OF HOW YOU WANT YOUR LIFE TO BE AND CREATE A ROADMAP TO GET THERE.

If you wanted to go to the Grand Canyon for vacation, there would be many steps to get there. You would need to make a decision to go there, know what the destination looks like, plan the route to get there, and set goals and milestones for you journey.

It also helps if you know someone who has been there before that can show you the way. You need to have a vision of where you are going with your life in order to get where you want to go.

Dream Big – Create Four Big Five-Year Goals From Your Future Vision

Your five-year goal could be to quit your job, have all your expenses paid for by passive income, and be able to travel the world. Another goal could be to have your children's college fund completely funded and buy a new house.

When you are setting your five-year goals, try use your vision of how you want your life to be and create a roadmap to get there. Whatever you put your mind to and stay hungry trying to attain the goals you will be able to achieve them.

You could have other goals like saving $30,000 in the bank by the five-year mark. It could be that in order to quit your job, you need to have some savings as a buffer for when things don't go exactly as planned.

Another goal could be that you want to be the healthiest and fittest you have even been in your life in five years. These can both be quantifiable and measurable.

Set Specific and Measurable Goals for Yourself

The purpose of goals is to help you attain what you desire. Make it specific, like hiking Half Dome in the Yosemite National Forest, or retiring in five years.

If I were to have the vision of being the healthiest and fittest ever in my life, I could find the basis to start from. To reach my goal, I must beat my previous benchmarks I already have for myself. Once I beat these, I have attained my goal.

Set Goals You Can Achieve with Maximum Effort

The saying "shoot for the moon" applies well to goal setting for your life. No, you don't want to set the expectations so high you cannot ever attain them, but you want them to be high enough to where you can get off the ground AND make it as close as you can to the moon.

Try to make goals that are hard for you to attain but not so hard that you cannot do it. Goals should be ones that you must continually work on in order to achieve them.

Set a Deadline for When the Five-Year Goals Must Be Accomplished

When you create your five-year goals, put a deadline on them to be completed. It is easiest to use either the first of the year or the date that you created your list of goals.

Either way, you have a fixed amount of time to accomplish your goals and it becomes more real to you. Think of it as a work deadline that you must finish. The "future" you is the boss and the "now" you is the employee.

Get Accountable

Reaching your goals is a hard thing to do. Life's circumstances get in the way, and things happen that throw you off the path. Having someone there holding you accountable to achieving your goals is a huge kick-in-the-pants to stay on track.

Find an accountability partner who is like minded in setting goals. They don't have to have the same goals, but they must be as serious as you are about having, working toward, and attaining their goals.

I suggest meeting or talking to your accountability partner weekly or biweekly, checking on each other, encouraging each other, and pushing each other along toward your destination.

Taking Action for Phase 2.2

➤ If you are currently renting a home to live in, strongly consider buying a home to live in. You will be able to capture most of these amazing benefits just by owning your own home.

  o Go to www.Zillow.com to look for properties in your area that you may be able to live in.

  o Look for 3 bedroom, 2 bathroom homes that are around 1400 square feet.

  o The price doesn't matter at this time. We will learn all about the valuation in a future chapter.

  o Keep this in mind. This is a property that will potentially be a rental in the future. You can keep trading up when you buy a new home and rent out your current one.

➤ If you already own your home, consider these investing options:

  o Think about refinancing your home to a lower interest rate to save you money. You will also be able to take out some of the equity you have in your home to buy another property.

  o Consider buying a new home for you to live in. If you are able to do that, you will be have your current home as a rental making you money each month.

PHASE 2.3

HOW TO THINK LIKE A RICH PERSON

In this phase, you are going to learn how you too can be rich just like Warren Buffet, Donald Trump, and Bill Gates by learning the ways that made them rich. They do not have different rules than us, they just know how to use the rules to their advantage.

She slowly walked into the living room as she was holding a piece of paper in her hand. My new bride of 6 months was noticeably irritated about something. My mind raced to think of what it could be.

Being the numbers person of the family, she had been going over our finances. We didn't have much money even with my job. My room mates moved out so there went the their rent and now I had to support my wife.

Questions ran through my mind like: "Did I forget to pay a bill?" and "Did we not have enough money to pay the mortgage?" Being that she moved from Arizona to live with me in California, she hadn't found a job until recently.

"I can't believe it" she exclaimed.

"What, what happened? Everything ok" I asked?

"Yes, everything is fine but can you believe the California government" she asked?

"Um, what's up" I asked?

"I can't believe how horrible taxes are here in California. I just received my first paycheck from my new job here in California and the taxes are so ridiculous" she said.

"Well, there are taxes in Arizona so what's the difference" I asked.

"In Arizona, I made more money per hour. Actually like $9 more per hour than I make here in California. You would think that the total dollar amount of taxes would be less here in California right" she asked?

"Sure, you made more total money from your job in Arizona than you are in California. What's the problem" I asked?

"Even though my check in California is $400 less than I was making in Arizona, there is MORE money taken out in taxes in California! Not just a little but a lot more total dollars were taken out from my California paycheck where I made $400 less than Arizona" she exclaimed!

Needless to say, this is just one of the reasons we moved out of California 11 years later. But the main point is that even though you work hard at your J.O.B., you are penalized by the government for working a J.O.B..

You are penalized in the form of taxes in your J.O.B. and it shows up in your paycheck. Now all states and cities have different tax rates but the one thing that is consistent, if you work a J.O.B., you are taxed more than investors like Warren Buffet, Donald Trump, and myself.

This is because we don't work for money. We have our money

work for us. Instead of having a J.O.B., we pay others to work and buy investments that make us money. In both cases, we are taxed differently than a hourly wage employee.

NO MORE TRADING HOURS
FOR DOLLARS

Most employees feel they are worth more than they are being paid which leads to a sense of entitlement. Remember J.O.B. = Just Over Broke.

If you have only one job, usually you are only able to work 40 hours a week for one employer, and your hourly wage is typically fixed unless you are on a commission. Let's look at some of the problems with trying to become rich as an employee.

1. As an employee you trade your hours for the employer's dollars, so you are stuck with whatever the employer decides to pay you. If you will not work for the pay, the employer will find someone else to do the job and pay them instead.

2. Everyone has limited time to give to a job. Attempting to work five jobs 40 hours a week at each one is physically impossible. There are not enough hours in the week to give, and you would not have the ability to perform as your boss expects.

3. Employees are a commodity for business owners. Just like any other commodity, it is supply and demand. If you work for Google, your job skills for the position are such that very few people can do what you can do. Your wage will probably be much higher than the normal wage because there are less people who can do your job. If you work for

McDonald's, you will probably be making the minimum wage because there are many others who can do the same work as you.

4. The IRS takes around 35% of your wages from you before you can even cash your check. Then if you consider state tax and sales tax, the total taxes you could be paying as an employee can be up to 50% of your wages. Just like that, half your money is gone!

5. The biggest problem of them all is, once you stop working, you stop being paid. If you were laid off or fired from your job, how would you pay for your expenses?

PRACTICAL STEPS TO ACHIEVING THE GOAL OF QUITTING YOUR J.O.B.

Start with the End in View

Dream big and create your five-year goals and work backwards from there. Start with creating your five-year goals.

- Where do you want to be?

- How many rental properties do you want to own?

- Do you want to quit your job?

- How much money do you want to have saved for when you quit your job?

- Make a list of all these five-year goals.

Create One-Year Milestones from Your Five-Year Goals

If you want to own 15 rental properties in 5 years, how would you go about doing it? You wouldn't be able to buy eight the first year, right?

How about starting small and as you build year after year; your momentum gains and you can do more in year five than you did in year one. See the blog post on: "How to Retire in 5 Years"

- Year one: Buy 1 rental property

- Year two: Buy 2 rental properties

- Year three: Buy 3 rental properties

- Year four: Buy 4 rental properties

- Year five: Buy 5 Rental properties

Each goal should have yearly milestones and monthly, weekly, and daily action steps for each goal. With a general five-year goal, life gets in the way, and by the time you realize it, you are in the second year without any action taken on your five-year plan.

Now you only have four years to do what you originally had five years to accomplish. Work on your goals daily so you can successfully reach them in the time frame you set for yourself.

Create Short Range Goals From Your One-Year Milestones

These should be specific action steps you can take to accomplish these one-year goals. If your desire is to save up $30,000 in 5 years you can do it by either cutting expenses or increasing revenue.

You may cut expenses and save $6,000 per year from your salary. Or start a small service business being a handyman to increase your annual income by $6,000 dollars and save that amount.

Each yearly goal should hopefully build on itself. After time, your small service business may not be so small because of advertising, word of mouth, etc. It may be bringing in much more money which would allow you to save the $30,000 faster AND buy more properties faster. All while beating your deadline by a couple years!

Read or Rewrite Your Goals Everyday

If you can't remember your goals, how well do you think you will accomplish them? Keep your goals on the forefront of your mind so you know exactly where you are in the process, what you need to do next, where you are deficient, and how to proceed.

Spend At Least 30 Minutes Each Day Working On Your Goals

Do anything that will help you reach your goals daily. If you wait all week to take the action steps on Friday what should have been done on Tuesday, you are almost setting yourself up for failure.

Get the most important things done at the start of the day, week, month, and year so you are not up against the deadline as time runs away from you.

Do Your Best to Not Move Your Deadline

I'm sorry to do this to you, but imagine this scenario: You are back in your senior year of high school and the final paper/ report assignment is due tomorrow morning at 9:00 am. You had all semester to research, draft, write, proofread, and finalize the report but you put it off until the day before, and now it is crunch time. Get it done, or fail the class.

Isn't it interesting that when our backs are up against the wall, we are capable of doing wonderful things in almost unrealistic timelines? Remember, you set these goals for yourself, and you also set the deadline for when these goals are to be accomplished. When you move a deadline that you create for yourself a couple things happen.

❖ You remove your ability to hunker down and get things done as you did when you were in high school with the report deadline.

❖ You give yourself permission to fail.

❖ You set yourself up to move the deadline again, and again, and again.

TRADITIONAL EDUCATION IS TEACHING YOU HOW TO BE AN EMPLOYEE

When we are young, we are all told to go to school and get good grades. Then we are to go to college and get a degree. Once completed, we are told to go find a job and get a pension, IRA, 401k, and we will be able to stop working when we are 65 years old.

Being an employee is a very honorable career, and for the majority of society this is a perfect fit for them. The government schools do not teach us how to be rich but rather how to take orders and be an employee.

We are taught to carry out the orders with a defined answer from the teacher's questions. To have financial freedom, we need to educate ourselves and learn from those who are already rich.

Those who want to be rich need to educate themselves to think like the rich because the rules of life are not different for them. Some may say that the rich in America have different rules than the middle or lower classes, but that is not the case.

In America, as there is equal justice under the law, there is also equal opportunity to be rich. The only way to be rich is to learn how to use the rules to play the game as the rich do. They have the same rules but they know how to use those rules to their advantage.

It has been stated that Warren Buffet, the billionaire investor, pays less in taxes than his secretary. He actually pays a lower tax rate than his secretary, which is different than total tax dollars.

In 2012, Warren Buffet paid a capital gains tax rate of 17.4% and his secretary paid an income tax rate of 35.8%. They both live under the same tax laws, but Warren chooses to make his money in a way that is taxed half as much as his secretary. His secretary is using everything she learned in school to be the best secretary for her boss, but the government still takes twice as much out of her paycheck than Warren Buffet.

This is because his income is earned as passive income. Passive Income is taxed as capital gains which has a lower tax rate (17.4%) than earned income (35.8%).

Following the example of the rich, you can use the laws to your benefit as they do:

1. Pay less in taxes and keep more of their money to spend however they want
2. Invest passive streams of income with cash flow every month
3. Quit working and stop paying outrageous income tax rates.

4. Stop trading hours for dollars
5. Your money works for you while you enjoy its fruits
6. Financial independence
7. You can leave a legacy to your loved ones
8. The ability to give more and more to those who are in need

The reason why it seems as though the rich have it easier than you is because they have learned how to play the game and use the laws to help them get rich.

TO BE SUCCESSFUL, YOU NEED TO BE EDUCATED LIKE THE RICH

In Robert Kiyosaki's book Cashflow Quadrant he teaches the four ways people make money: Employee, Sole Proprietor, Business Owner, and Investor.

Active	Passive
E	**B**
Employee	Business Owner
S	**I**
Self-Employed	Investor

E's and S's
Left side of the Cashflow Quadrant

Employee

Desires job security, a steady paycheck, no financial risk, and the benefits provided by their jobs (retirement, insurance, time off, sick days, etc.).

Sense of entitlement is high with the employee, and they trade hours for dollars. They also pay the highest tax rate.

Sole Proprietor

Is their own boss and are not dependent upon other people for their financial security. These include doctors, lawyers, and anyone who is self-employed.

They desire independence and tend to be controlling, not trusting others to do the work as good as they can. Their income is tied directly to how much they work and if they do not work, they don't get paid. They basically "own" a job.

B's and I's

Right side of the cashflow quadrant:

Business Owner

Starts businesses and hire employees to delegate as much as possible. They work "on" the business and find competent people to work "in" the business. They desire to create a business that can run on its own without them. They focus on creating systems for the business to make money without them.

Investor

Looks for ways to make their money, as well as the money of others, work for them. They desire to work less so they can spend their time however they want while not being tied down to a job.

Escapes high taxes by deferring their taxes to a future date or utilizes the IRS rules to pay the lowest tax rate of all the other groups. They receive 70% of their income from investments and less than 30% from a job.

If you want to be rich, you should move to the B and I side of the Cashflow Quadrant ASAP

The rich focus the majority of their efforts on the Business and Investor side of the Cashflow Quadrant because that is where the real wealth and money is. The good news is, if you are starting in the Employee category you can move to any of the other quadrants at any given time. It IS entirely possible to move from E to I very quickly.

Here are some of the benefits of being on the right side of the cashflow quadrant.

1. Every dollar you invest is another employee working for you who makes more employees who do the same
2. Live wherever they want
3. Do whatever they want
4. Buy whatever they want
5. Income comes in the mail whether they work 60 hours a week or 1

6. Complete financial freedom

7. Pay lowest of all tax rates

8. Defer taxes to a future date with IRS 1031 exchanges almost indefinitely

9. No liability because corporations own everything

10. Complete control over everything because they own the corporations

11. Not dependent on anyone for their lifestyle or freedom

12. As soon as their income from investments surpass their wages, they retire

13. Not dependent on Social Security, 401K, IRA, Pension, etc.

Taking Action for Phase 2.3

➢ Commit to changing your way of thinking from an employee who trades dollars for hours to an investor gets paid by the value that you can produce.

➢ Get started now.

    o If you have not done it yet, take 15-20 minutes to consider and write down your 5 year goals. Really think them through and get them on paper.

    o Take 15 minutes to figure out your yearly milestones.

    o Plan how you will get out of the Left Side of the Cashflow Quadrant to the Right Side

PHASE **3**

Build A Strong Structure

PHASE 3.1

MAKE YOUR MONEY WORK FOR YOU, NOT YOU FOR MONEY

"If you don't find a way to make money while you sleep, you will work until you die."

- Warren Buffet

"Hey Babe, we just made an extra $350 this month!" I shouted to my wife with excitement.

"How did we do that?" She asked.

"The rental property we bought is now rented and we are making money!" I explained.

"Oh terrific! I am so relieved that this rental property business seems to be actually working out" she said.

"Yes and this is just the start of the business with one property. Imagine if we had 5 properties that brought in $350 a month. That would be $1,750 a month in passive income" I exclaimed!

"That would be such a huge blessing, wouldn't it" she asked?

"It sure would be! What if we had 10, 20, or even 30 properties making that much? I wouldn't even need to work a job anymore!" I said.

"We'll have to keep growing the business but just make sure we don't grow too fast. This passive income thing is amazing but I don't want us to get in over our heads" she said.

Well, 10 years and 35 properties, we are doing very well. Since I will never stop buying properties, the income will only go up. The money we invest in a rental property is basically like a little employee working for us. Now, we have millions of little employees working for us, making us money every minute of every day. Even when we sleep, we are still making money.

HAVE YOUR DOLLARS BE LIKE EMPLOYEES, WORKING 24 HOURS A DAY, 7 DAYS A WEEK

Passive income in monthly cash flow through real estate is truly passive. You are not working for a J.O.B. where you clock in or out, but you are working on your own business. With real estate, property managers are my best friends.

I hire the best property manager because I want the best manager looking after my properties making me the most money while I sit back and get my monthly statement in the mail with a fat rent check. My property manager does all the work, gets compensated well, and I just make money.

By owning just one single family home with tenants who pay you monthly rent to live there, you are bringing in $300-$400 a month in passive income. You buy the home once, and your house is working for you 24 hours a day, 7 days a week.

Whether you are in Hawaii or camping in the mountains, your property is working hard at making you money every minute of every day. Now imagine you had 10 properties that brought in the same amount of money each month, minus expenses. This would bring you $3,000 to $4,000 a month in passive income.

Here is the general math for one property with easy round numbers:

Rental Home on 321 Main St.
Purchase Price: $100,000

Monthly Expenses	Monthly Income
Mortgage: $536 (5% note at 30 years)	Rents Collected: $1100
Taxes & Insurance: $175	Net Operating Income (NOI): ($1,100-$175)=$925
Total Monthly Expenses: $711	Total Profit (Income - Expenses): $389

This home on 321 Main St. would bring you $389 a month in cash flow from passive income! Now, imagine you owned 10 of these properties bringing in $389 a month in passive cash flow.

This equates to $3,339 in your pocket every month without you doing any work since your money is doing the work. Now, imagine how your life would be if you owned 100 of these properties. Your income would be $33,390 a month in passive cash flow!

THE PLAN

HOW TO QUIT YOUR J.O.B. IN FIVE YEARS

"If you fail to plan, you are planning to fail."

−Benjamin Franklin

In order to understand what it would take for you to retire from your job, you need to know what your expenses are. By knowing your expenses, you will have a target income needed to live off of. If you have not completed the budget in from earlier, do so now.

Find the total expenses that you have and that will give you the total dollar amount that you need in order to quit your job. The total I needed was $4,000 a month from passive income for my family and me to live securely and not need my job. Once I found my number I was able to plan out my future investing career.

Now, let's work on how you can do the same thing, too.

Step 1: Find Your Target Income Amount

From the budget you created in the last chapter, write down your total monthly expenses. This is your benchmark dollar amount you must get to in order to not need a J.O.B. to pay your bills. Once you acquire enough rental properties to pay for these expenses, you really don't need a job.

Let's say that you have $3,800 in expenses every month, and you want to quit your job and have enough income to pay your mortgage, bills, travel expenses, etc.

Step 2: Determine How You Will Invest

Now, think of what it would take to attain $4,000 in monthly passive income in monthly cash flow. It could be that in the next 5 years you buy a total of 15 properties that make you $300 a month in passive income in monthly cash flow.

There are many different types of properties that will bring you this kind of return on your money. A good rule of thumb is to stick with properties that people in the market you are investing in would want to rent.

I personally stay away from two bedroom homes. They are harder to rent, the prices are almost as high, and the rents are much less. I suggest sticking with a cookie-cutter type of home.

Property Type: $100,000 Single Family Home	Property Type: $40,000 Single Family Home
B or C quality home Purchase Price of $100,000 3 bedroom 2 bathroom 2 car garage 1,400+ sqft Built after 1980 Rents for $1,100	C or D quality home Purchase Price of $40,000 3 bedroom 2 bathroom 2 car garage 1,200+ sqft Built after 1950 Rents for $750

With these two types of properties, you will have a good chance of getting a good return on your money. With interest rates being at or around 3%, the expenses and the mortgage payment would be much less than the rent, and you would get passive income in cash flow each month.

Step 3: Know How Many Properties You Need to Pay for All Your Expenses

To retire in 5 years with your expenses at $4,000, your yearly plan could look like this:

Year 1: Buy one single family home with $300 monthly income

Year 2: Buy two single family homes with $300 monthly income

Year 3: Buy three single family homes with $300 monthly income

Year 4: Buy four single family homes with $300 monthly income

Year 5: Buy five single family homes with $300 monthly income

At year 5, you have 15 single family homes with $300 a month coming in. That would be $4,500 a month in passive cash flow!

Imagine what you could do with $4,500 a month! You could pay your expenses and have extra money to spend on whatever you want! If you continue on that path of adding more properties to your investment portfolio, you double, triple, or even make ten times that each month!

Now, you may be thinking that buying properties in that example is impossible. Believe me, it is not. I have done it, and so can you! In 6 years I bought 19 single family homes that bring in $400 or more a month in passive income. Plus I did all this while having a full time job and a full time family.

Everyone's circumstances are different. Where they start, how they build their business, and how they end. All of my students that I coach how to invest in real estate have different situations and circumstances that we work through to help them attain their goal. A big part of my coaching is figuring out a plan to help them get to their goal with where they are currently.

Lots of Debt, low or no income, lack of investing knowledge, no finances, no savings, etc. are all things that my students have all overcame in order to change their lives.

Wherever your financial situation is, there is a way out. It will take work, but if you push through it, you can build a successful real estate business.

If you learn how to invest in rental properties, you will have the passive income you need to reach your goals.

Right now, buying 15 properties in 5 years sounds pretty daunting but you CAN do it! There are so many different ways to purchase rental properties that you will have no issue with finding them.

If you learn some of the advanced techniques, you can even buy them with no money out of your pocket. In the next chapters, you will learn all the steps needed to earn passive income from rental properties and quit your job!

Taking Action for Phase 3.1

➢ Go to www.Zillow.com and look at the surrounding areas of your city for other places to invest. Look for properties that match the criteria we already discussed. 3 bedroom, 2 bathroom, 1400 square feet.

➢ Start and Excel worksheet to keep track of all the properties that catch your eye and seem to meet your criteria. Keep this sheet as a record of the following characteristics of the properties:

   o Address, Asking Price, Bedrooms, Bathrooms, Rental Estimate

PHASE 3.2

PRINCIPLES TO INVESET ANYWHERE IN THE WORLD

Recently I got an email question from one of my podcast listeners. Actually, this is the same as many others who listen to my podcast, read my investing articles, and from those who read my books.

> "Hey Dustin. I came across your podcast this past month and it has opened my eyes and inspired me to take a similar path in life to you. It seems we have a lot of similarities in How we want to spend our time and how valuable family time is! I have owned a barbershop in Halifax NS, in Canada for the past 3 years and have always been interested in rental properties to create passive income.
>
> I live in Canada and hope that your methods work similar in this Country. I'm very thankful for all your advice Dustin!"

Because I live in America, people tend to think that investing in real estate doesn't work outside the USA. This is not true at all. Real estate investing can be done anywhere in the world. There are only two caveats to this:

1. Places where you cannot own property.
2. Places were people do not want to live.

The former would be very bad places where thieves, military dictators, socialist governments and others can and will just take your property from you. The beauty about America and most of the western world is the freedom to own property without concern that someone will take it by force.

The latter would be places like in the middle of the desert, or in the middle of a swamp. Places like this have a very limited amount of people that would actually rent from you. Also, you would have a hard time getting financing for these properties as well. Banks are very hesitant to lend in places that people do not live.

Investing in real estate rental properties is basically the same throughout the entire world. It doesn't matter the country as long as you follow these principles.

Always Make A Positive Monthly Return Of Cash Flow Each Month

At the top of the list, and I mean the #1 reason for investing in real estate, is making a positive cash flow each month from the rents received. The equation for this is super simple. Actually, I am teaching this to my 7 year-old and he get's it.

Example:
A 3 bedroom, 2 bathroom home has monthly rents for $1,200 and has $850 in total monthly expenses.

Income – Expenses = Profit
$1,200 - $850 = $350

Cash flow means money coming in or out of your pocket. Positive cash flow puts money in your pocket and negative cash flow takes money out. From the equation above, if you owned this property, you would make a positive cash flow of $350. That is $350 more a month coming into your pocket!

Monthly cash flow is the reason why rental property owners make money no matter what happens in the real estate market. The market can go up, down, or sideways and the rental property will still make money each month.

Even if the market crashes and the property value drops in half, my properties still make me money. The reason why I will always make money in every market is: There will always be renters since everyone needs a place to live and I am happy to give them the ability to rent a nice home where I make money every month.

Buy Lower than Market Value

There is a phrase I want you to learn: You make your money when you buy the property. You realize your money when you sell the property.

> You make your money when you buy the property.
>
> You realize your money when you sell the property.
>
> Buy Low / Sell High

As in the stock market, if you buy low and sell high, you make money. Imagine buying Amazon stock at $250 a share when they first went public. Over time, as the company does well and grows, the value of that stock goes up.

Now, imagine selling the Amazon stock for $750. You just made a profit of $500. This is the sale price, less the purchase price, and this gives you your profit. $750 - $250 = $500 in profit.

The same goes for real estate. As an investor, you want to buy low and sell high. BUT, I'll do one even better! Imagine buying Amazon stock at a discount? Instead of $250, you pay $200, $175, or $100 for the same stock. That stock would be heavily discounted even though you know the value of the stock is actually $250! This is exactly what you can do with real estate.

In real estate, it is absolutely possible to buy a property for lower than the actual value of the property. In fact, EVERY property I purchase is worth much more than I bought it for. When you do this, you capture equity on the first day you buy the property.

One property I purchased in Houston was worth $225,000 at the time. I bought it for $151,000. The property needed work and I put in $22,000 to get it rented. That is $173,000 total to get the property.

$225,000 - $173,000 = $52,000 profit!

That is a $52,000 profit on the property captured in equity in the property. If I were to sell it, that is how much I would be able to sell it for and profit not including fees. As investors though, we don't flip homes, we rent for cash flow. At some point in the future, I will sell this home to trade it up and buy apartment complexes.

Buy Properties You Can Fix Up and Force Up Appreciation

When I buy properties, I buy them so that I can make money by fixing up the property to make it nicer for someone to live in. I never buy the best house on the street. I buy the best investment on the street that I can add value to it by fixing up the property.

You want to buy properties that you can invest your money

into to fix it up. After it is fixed up, you will have an increase in property value because of the new updates.

Make Sure the Expenses are Lower than the Rental Income

Income must be more than your expenses in order to make money every month from the rents.

Pro Tip: Always go back and analyze your expenses to see if you can lower them. At least once a year, go over all your expenses and make sure you have cut as many of the costs out of your expenses.

Here are some ideas where you can look for expenses to cut:

- Insurance
- Lower property taxes,
- Find a new property manager,
- Electric company, etc.

Increase Your Rental Income

Once a year, you should look at all of the properties for a potential rental price increase. Most homes are on a yearly lease. A lease is good for both the landlord and the renter. It is good for the landlord because it locks the tenant in for one year. It is also good for the tenant because it locks them in the property for one year and keeps the price of rent the same for the one year.

Once the lease is up, look to increase the rent 5% to 10%. I personally would not go any more than that. The only reason why I would, would be to get the tenant out of the report sooner than they may want to leave.

If you need to raise the rents up 30% to catch up to market rents, it would be a good idea to do so slowly over time. 5% here, 10% there, and over time, you will be up to market rents.

Pro Tip: If you are raising rents, let the tenant know that the market rents are 30% more than they are paying. Because you are understanding and want to take care of them, you are only going to raise it up 7.5% every year until you get to the market rents. This gives you your increase and allows the tenant to adjust for the rent increase or move out.

Make Sure There Is Enough Demand For Your Property

When you are looking for a place to invest, take your time to make sure to inspect all aspects of the area. Inspect the city, community, neighborhood and street to ensure there is demand for your properties. Again, if you buy in the middle of the desert, there may not be many people that would rent your place.

Only Invest Where People Will Rent Your Property

If the demand is low for your rental, you will get low rents for it because of high supply and low demand. You want to get top dollar for your property. If you are renting in an area that has problems with it, you will run into issues.

Things to look out for: Crime, poor schools, industrial, commercial sites, etc. These are not the best places for people to live so less people want to rent there.

Pro Tip: Look at the movement of crime throughout the area. Crime moves locations so see the trend and the path it is going. Make sure you are not in the path of future crime.

One area of the country I invested in 10 years ago was a good area. The crime was in the south west area of the city and I was investing in the far south east area. It was a good area 10 years ago but over time, the crime moved from the west to the east. Now that area is a rough area. Harder to find good tenants in rougher areas.

Buy Good Investments, NOT Good Properties

A good investment will make you monthly cash flow from the rents. A good property is, the nicest on the block, needs no work, is worth more than others in the area. This is NOT what you want. You want a property that you can pay lower than market value for, fix up, and increase the value.

A good investment will make you money. A good property may cost you more money and your income will be lower. A good property is one that you want to live in, not rent out to a tenant. Remember, each property is another piece of inventory in your business. Think of them as inventory and not a home you will be living in.

Place Good Tenants and Run Background Checks

When I first started, I never did a background check. Man was I wrong. I lost so much money because I didn't really know the history of the tenant I was placing in my property. Your goal is to keep a tenant in your property for as long as possible. The longer they are in there the more money you make.

Once I got smart and started doing background checks, I found my income stabilized, fewer evictions occurred, and I was making a lot more money. Good tenants are out there, you just need to wait until one comes to you to live in your property.

After I started doing background checks, I found a potential tenant was evicted 4 times in 3 years. Her application looked great. Good rental history, good income, good everything. But, she was lying. Needless to say, I did not allow her to rent my property.

Make the Property Rent Ready, NOT the Best House On the Street

If you make the property the best property, you may have spent too much money fixing it up. When the other properties in your area do not have granite countertops, you may not need to spend that money to get a good tenant. You may even be adding in extra costs to your fixup that you did not need.

You want your investment to bring back as much money as possible into your pocket with the least amount of money out of it. As you are going through the process of fixing up the property, make sure you keep asking the question: "Will what I'm doing to the property make me more money in the end"? If the answer is no, then consider leaving it out.

Buy Properties that Make You $250 or More Each Month in Passive Income

There is a great reason why you want to make $250 or more, it is because you want to make as much money as possible. Right?!

Of course you do. Well, if you didn't account for possible unexpected expenses, you may run a negative.

If you don't make $250 a month in passive income, one large issue will cost you your entire years' worth of profit. If a furnace would go out, you may need to replace it. That cost alone could be $3,000-$5,000.

With only making $100 a month in profit, you would only make $1,200 a year. It would take you at least 2 years at $100 a month in profit to pay for the new furnace. If you made $250 a month, you would make $3,000 in one year which would be much easier to help pay for the new furnace. Make sure you make enough money each month to turn a profit every year.

Run your business like a business

As soon as you own one rental property, you now own a business. Even if it is a small one, it is still a business. On top of getting all the tax benefits of having a business, you get the benefit of acting like a business.

This may sound like common sense but you would be surprised how many people do not treat their business like a business. I, like just about every other investor who started on their own, made the mistake of the same thing. Not running the business as a business.

Let me give you an example:

What would happen if you stopped paying your mortgage to the bank for the home you live in? Would they be a pushover and allow you to get by with making half payments, missing deadlines, and allow you to live in the property without starting the foreclosure process? Absolutely not. The second you missed a payment, or made a half payment, they would start the process of foreclosure as documented in the note you signed when you got your mortgage.

The bank is running like a business when they follow the rules. These rules were put in place when they gave you the loan and you got the keys to your new house. Once the transaction is finished, it now depends on business decisions from this point out.

If a bank, running like a business, would not let you stay in the property one second longer than you paid for, then why would you allow a tenant stay in the property a second longer than they have paid for? The answer is, you shouldn't. Running your business like a business is where you set up AND follow the business rules you put in place. Let me give you an example of rules to follow:

> Running your business like a business is where you set up AND follow the business rules you put in place.

1. Rent is due on the 1st

2. Rent is late after the 3rd with a late fee

3. On the 3rd, a 3-day notice to pay or vacate is put on the door

4. 3 days later, the eviction is filed with the local court

5. The eviction process, once started, will not stop until it is finished or the tenant pays for all the back rent, late fees, court fees, lawyer fees, along with any and all other fees.

6. Do not accept any money unless it is in full. Any money received will cause the eviction process to stop.

7. File a Writ with the court and meet the Sheriff Deputy at the property to remove the tenant and their belongings.

This is what I mean by running your business as a business. Set up business rules and processes in your business and follow them. Don't be lenient unless you absolutely must. When you are lenient, the tenant will consider you a lenient landlord and will continue to push the limits of your leniency.

I've personally lost tens of thousands of dollars by not following these, and other rules like this. One tenant stayed in the property for 3 months before I started the eviction. This took another 2 months to complete. When it was all done, the tenant was in the property for almost 6 months without paying rent.

Make sure you run your business like a business.

Taking Action for Phase 3.2

➤ Take time to write down the business processes and procedures you should have in your business. Even if you do not have any properties now, answer these questions and put them in writing so you have them to refer to when you come across these things in your business.

1. What are the due, late, and eviction dates for your properties?

2. What are the late fees you are going to charge?

3. What will you do with partial payments?

4. What will you do when a tenant tells you they will get paid in two Fridays and they need you to wait until then to get paid?

5. How will you handle the eviction process? Will you or a property manager go through with the process?

6. Will you overpay for a property or fight to get the purchase price as low as possible?

7. If there is a major repair, will you only get one, two, or three or more quotes to get the lowest price?

8. What dollar amount will be fine for your property manager to spend without your approval?

9. Will you allow tenants to work on the property and deduct it from the rent?

10. Will you inspect the property any time during the lease?

11. Will you increase the rents upon the lease renewal?

12. How will you handle complaints from the local government?

There are many other questions that you will have to come up with and answer yourself. Always err on the side of running your business as a business. Remember, this business is how you will feed your family and pay your bills. Don't be a pushover and let your tenants get away with things you would never be able to get away with.

PHASE 3.3

UNDERSTANDING THE PROCESS OF TURNING A REAL ESTATE TRANSACTION INTO CASH FLOW

"Are you sure this is the right thing to do" my wife asked me one day?

"Absolutely babe, this is the right thing to do" I replied.

"Well, how do you actually make money in this? I mean, I understand that you rent out the property to tenants, but you haven't even bought the property yet" she said.

"The process is simple" I said to her. "The process has a few steps but they are easily handled. I have a realtor, title company, property manager, contractors, etc. all ready to help me through the process of turning this property into a money making business."

"I understand that you know the process, but you are spending all of our savings on this property that could potentially be a money pit. If you want me to be on board, you need to explain the entire process" she said.

This was the scene in my kitchen as I was buying my first property. Even though I had done all the research needed to get started, I still needed to convince my wife AND teach her the entire business from scratch. She wanted to have her fear of losing everything with knowledge of the business.

As I walked her through the entire business, things really came to light that I didn't really know everything about the process. Holes were found, items missed, and working with my wife, we did our best to fix all the issues we had in the process.

I would say that this is the way for half of the coaching students I have as I teach them real estate investing. More often than not, one spouse is fully bought in while the other spouse is much more unsure and even resistant. What it comes down to for those who are unsure and resistant is lack of knowledge.

As my wife and I worked together through the process, I was able to educate her on the real estate process to cash flow. She eventually, after lots of explaining, approved of the business and we bought our first property. Now, 35 properties and growing, she has no worries about the business and doesn't even think about it.

Recently, I purchased three single family homes and a duplex from another investor. This was a great deal. $25,000 cash with the rest in a seller financed note. With the note payment and all the other expenses, I make $1,600 a month in rent. Once the note payment is paid off, I'll be making $2,300 a month from this purchase.

The great thing was that I didn't even tell my wife I was doing it. I came home one day from finishing the transaction with the seller to be with my family. My wife asked me how my day was and I said to her, "Great, I just bought three single family homes and a duplex! We will make $1,600 a month in rent!"

"Wow, that's great honey. Good job! Well, diner is almost ready" she said.

And that was it. I no longer needed to help her understand the business or even let her know what was going on. Since we are making tens of thousands of dollars each month, and a great track record of 10 years of business success, she does not even think about the business.

Now, let me walk you through the process of a real estate transaction to cash flow.

UNDERSTANDING THE PROCESS OF TURNING A REAL ESTATE TRANSACTION INTO CASH FLOW

Now we are going to look at how you buy a rental property from beginning to end step by step. The process is not complicated but there are many steps to understand and follow.

It is important to follow each step and learn the process included in each one of the steps in order to not lose money on a deal. We will start from the very beginning of the process to the end where you are making money every single month with passive income from the rent received.

In this process, if a step is skipped, it may or may not be fine for you and your business. If you skip the title company step, you may end up with a home with a lean or back taxes on the property that you would have to pay for.

Here is a diagram of the process from beginning to end:

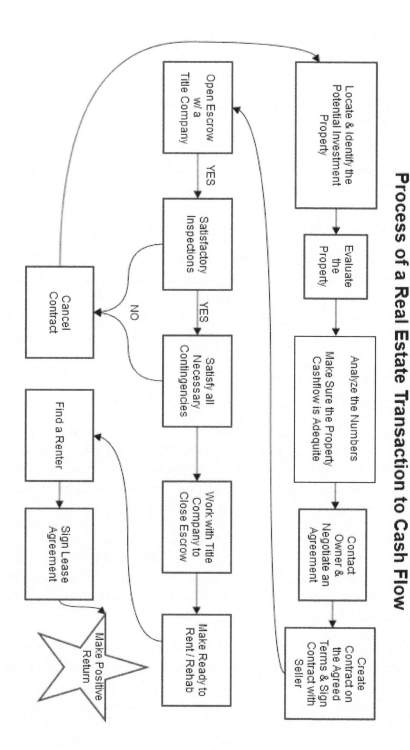

Process of a Real Estate Transaction to Cash Flow

Now let's look at each one of these individually and dig deeper to what these mean.

Locate and Identify the Potential Investment Property

The first step is to find a property among the hundreds that are currently listed for sale in the area where you would like to start investing. There are a few ways to start looking, but the quickest is to go to www.zillow.com and search for the type of property that could fit the criteria you are looking for.

I suggest looking for three bedroom two bath single-family homes, with over 1400 square feet and a two-car garage. The price range should be between $80,000-$120,000. These types of properties will rent well and bring in a good cash flow each month with the current interest rate that you can get with a single family home.

Evaluate the Property

Now, single-family homes are valued based upon comparable sales in the area of like properties. So to find the value of a property you are looking at, you want to find another home within a two mile radius of the subject property that has the same amount of bedrooms, bathrooms, and square footage.

By doing this you see what somebody else paid for the property and see if the asking price on your deal is a reasonable price or not. Zillow does a decent job at finding these comparable sales for you. It compares like homes to yours and gives you their opinion of what the value should be.

I have found that the Zillow values are on the high end, meaning they value the property a little higher than most appraisers would.

Remember one of the reasons why we buy real estate is that

we can buy a property below market value and instantly gain equity in the property. This is because we make <u>money</u> when we buy the property and we <u>realize</u> the money when we sell it. Obviously, it's best to get as much equity as you can out of the property when you buy it. That all depends on if the seller is going to sell it for less than market value.

What you need to do is negotiate with the seller and try to get them to accept an offer price less than the market value. I try shoot for 80% of the market value so I instantly gain 20% equity in the property.

The example below shows that if you buy a property with the market value of $120,000 for only $100,000 you will instantly make $20,000 in equity because you bought the property cheaper than what it was worth.

Market Value	$120,000
Asking Price	$118,000
Negotiated Purchase Price	$100,000
Money Made When you Bought the Property	$20,000

There are also other things that come into factor like the rehab costs which also eat into your equity because the purchase price plus the rehab costs equal the total amount to get the property rented. Your equity capture is the market value of the property minus the purchase price minus the rehab costs.

If you fix up the kitchen, flooring, bathrooms, paint the walls, and do other things that make the property worth more you will increase the value of the property.

The example below shows that if you buy a home for $100,000 and you put in $25,000 to fix it up, the new market value will go up. Depending on the market the value can go up quite significantly.

In this example you see the new market value is $180,000 because similar homes that are up-to-date like this one are selling for the same amount. The comparable sales of these other properties raise the value of your home because of the rehab you did on the home. With rehabbing the property you have forced the appreciation of equity to $55,000! This is on top of the monthly passive income you make each time the renter pays their rent.

New Market Value	$180,000
Purchase Price	- $100,000
Rehab Costs	- $25,000
New Equity from Forced Appreciation Through Rehab	$55,000

Analyze the Numbers and Make Sure the Property Cash Flows

This sounds like a hard thing to do, but in reality it is really only elementary school math at play here. The only caveat is if you can account for all of the expenses and income properly and anticipate future expenses that may eat into your cash flow.

What it comes down to is income minus expenses equals a positive or negative cash flow. If the property rents for $1000 per month and your expenses are $1200 per month, you will lose $200 each month just by owning the property because of negative cash flow.

Now if your property rents for $1000 a month and your expenses are only $750 per month, you make $250 per month positive cash flow.

There are many expenses that you will come across. Here is a list of a few you will encounter:

- Accounting
- Advertising
- Reserve funds
- Security services

- Electricity
- Insurance
- Management fees
- Lawn care

- Pest control
- Repairs
- Poverty taxes
- Utilities

It is important to make sure that you find all the expenses for the property itemized out so you can analyze the deal accurately and not buy a bad property. You can find my free Investment Property Calculator on my website which will do all the analysis of any deal for you.

http://www.masterpassiveincome.com/calculator

You also want to make sure that you understand what it's going to cost to fix up the property in order to get rented. You may want to bring in a few different contractors and get multiple bids for the repairs.

It is wise to know what it's going to cost to fix up the property before you buy it. Trained professionals like contractors know what to look for that a new investor would not know about.

Contact the Owner and Negotiate an Agreement with Them

This can be one of the more scary parts of the transaction process. It's always hard to approach someone you don't know and ask them if they would be willing to sell you their property for less than market value. But the more you do the easier it will get.

This is the part where your personality must come out and show them that you are a credible and honest person that is willing to help them in any way possible. If they are willing to sell, you need to agree on a few things and have them put into a contract.

These include purchase price, inspection period, escrow length, concessions, and/or contingencies, and other items that you discuss and agree to. The owner may be willing to carry a note on the property and basically be the banker and you pay them the mortgage each month. There are many other questions and items in the contract you need to discuss.

Create the Contract on the Agreed Upon Terms and the Contract with the Seller

Once you negotiated with the seller all the terms of the contract, you then need to write it up and have them sign it ASAP. By doing this, you are locking up the property so no one else can buy it from underneath you.

There are many different types of templates for contracts for buying and selling a property. I used a template I got off the Internet for the first property that I bought. It worked out just fine, and those contracts are easy to find. Check our resources page for sample contracts for you to use.

www.masterpassiveincome.com/resources

Open Escrow with a Title Company

Now it's time to get a third-party involved in the deal. A third-party is somebody that's impartial to the deal and has experience in the escrow process. There are many title companies that do this, and it's up to you to find one that you are the seller both can agree upon.

Escrow basically is where the title company receives your contract that is signed by both parties and holds both parties to said contract. The title company will then do a search for any liens or encumbrances against the property. They will make sure that the property does not have any obligations like an outstanding mortgage or overdue taxes.

If the title company signs off on the property, they issue you title insurance to cover any issues they may have missed while doing the search. This insurance is there to protect you in case the title company does not do the job right.

Satisfactory Inspections

Now that escrow is open it is time for you to start your inspections of the property to make sure that you're buying a sound property. Inspections that you will probably want to have done are: home inspection, termite inspection, flood inspection, roof inspection.

There are other inspections you can possibly do if you'd like, but these are the typical inspections you should do. There is an expense involved in doing these inspections, but in my opinion it's well worth it to do them.

I do not want to buy a property that I will have to put tens of thousands of dollars into it because I didn't pull out of the deal when I should have.

Satisfy All Necessary Contingencies

There may be contingencies that you and the seller agree to in the negotiation process. Some contingencies may include a financing contingency, insurance contingencies, selling of a current home, appraisal, and basically anything that you and the seller agree to.

You can ask for just about any type of contingency you want but it's up to the seller if they want to agree to those contingencies. It doesn't hurt to ask for a contingency if it might be necessary to have.

For example, if the property is in a flood or tornado zone it might be good to have a contingency stating that the sale is contingent on you being able to get adequate insurance for the property.

Work with the Title Company to Close Escrow

Once the title work has been done and no liens are against the property and all inspections and contingencies are accounted for, it is now time to sign the escrow papers that the title company creates. Both the seller and the buyer sign the escrow papers itemizing all of the closing costs as well as the terms of the deal.

That title company will then receive your money that you are required to pay the seller and distribute the proceeds of the sale to the seller. The title company will also create a deed of sale and record it with the local county recorder making the transaction public record for anyone to see.

Once the deed has been recorded the property is now yours and you are ready to start rehabbing the property. Make sure your contractors are ready to rehab the property the very day you get the property. Don't waste any time because time is money.

Make Ready – Rehab the Property

Now that you have the keys to the property, it is time for you to get in there and rehab it. If you doing the work yourself you will save a lot of money, but there is a lot more work on your shoulders to get done.

Doing the work yourself will also take longer than if you got a good contractor who will work on your property quickly and efficiently. A good contractor will work hard for you to get the property on the market and ready to rent as soon as possible.

Be sure to account for the rehab costs when you are buying the property so you don't run out of money before you have the ability to rent it.

Find a Renter

It is now time to put the property on the market for rent. There are many different ways to find renters. Depending on your market there are different ways for finding tenants. In some markets craigslist.com is the perfect way to find renters.

In other markets it is better to hire a realtor who matches a tenant to a property because that is the way the tenants find places to rent. Be sure to look at the market and take into account the proper amount of marketing budget you need for the property.

I always have my property managers find the tenants, show the property to them, sift through all the applications, and present the best options to me. I then have the final say, and I run a background and criminal check on all tenants that I choose to have live in my property.

In the past, I was cheap and tried to save $30 per tenant by not running the background, criminal, and eviction check. I eventually realized that by running these checks on prospective tenants, I am able to weed out tenants that would possibly move out of my property quickly. It is expensive to evict a tenant.

Here are some costs you may incur: eviction fees, attorney fees, writ fees, and cleaning up the property. Don't forget the loss of rents for that time that the property is not rented. I found that by spending $30 on a background check it saves me from many evictions that cost upwards of $1,000 to $1,500 in total costs.

I was so glad that I did a background, criminal, and eviction check on one lady who had been evicted four times in the last three years. That's $30 possibly saved me $1,500 in carrying costs, loss of rents, eviction fees, etc.

I strongly encourage you to always run a background, criminal, and eviction check on all possible tenants. Go to http://www.masterpassiveincome.com/resources/ to find good places to do background checks.

Sign the Lease Agreement with the Tenant

This is another item that I let my property manager take care of. He meets with the tenant, has them sign the lease, and pay the first month's rent and the security deposit. Once he has all this done, he gives the tenant the keys on the designated date of the move-in.

If they move-in in the middle of the month you prorate the rent for each day they lived there to the next month. So if they move in on June 15, there are 15 more days in the month for them to pay rent for.

If they are paying $700 a month for the rent, you divide the monthly rent($700) by the days in the month (30) days which gives you $23.33 per day. The daily rate times the amount of days the tenant will live there equals that month rent.

So 15 days times $23.33 equals $350 to move in with 15 days left in the month. Many times you will get tenants that are leaving their previous place they were living in on the thirty-first and move into yours on the first of the month.

Make a Positive Return on Your Money

If you followed these steps and bought the property right you will be making a monthly return on your investment. This is from the passive income from the rent received minus the expenses for the property. Remember that the monthly rents are only one part of six different ways that you can make money and it is the most important.

Taking Action for Phase 3.2

➢ Go to the www.MasterPassiveIncome.com/resources page and download the free sample contract to review. Read it over and be ready to fill it out on your first offer to purchase a house.

➢ Continue looking for properties on www.Zillow.com. Keep a record of the properties that interest you in the Excel spreadsheet you already created.

PHASE 4

FINISH WORK

PHASE 4.1

BUILD YOUR REAL ESTATE BUSINESS DREAM TEAM

"Teamwork is the ability to work together toward a common vision. The ability to direct individual accomplishments toward organizational objectives. It is the fuel that allows common people to attain uncommon results."

- Andrew Carnegie

The hallway was dark, wet, cold, and had a smell that was both old and familiar. Doors lined this cramp hallway leading to unknown rooms that held items we were both curious and excited to see. If these rooms could tell you their secrets of things past, one can only imagine what they would say.

The rain almost never stopped here. Day after day, the rain relentlessly pounded on the land. For this particular hallway, both the east and west entrance was exposed to the open air and the afternoon sky. The wind and rain funneled through this hallway making us even more cold than we were outside under the cloudy skies.

Soaking wet from the rain and shivering from the wind, we slowly walked into the hallway. As I lead my wife and four children down from room to room, we stopped at each door to look inside to see what each room held. Even though each room was the same size and shape, they all had different items from the past in them. Swords, armor, cannons, replica clothing and kids toys. What stood out to us the most was the last room.

This was not really a room, but a cave carved into the mountain of rock that the entire castle was built on. The last room in this hallway though was not like the others. This cave was where the enemies of king would be held, tortured, and eventually killed.

Chains and shackles were attached to the walls to hang the prisoners, instruments of torture lined the walls, and an uneasy feeling crept over all of us in the room. Seeing a place like this that was built thousands of years ago was just awe inspiring. Castle Edinburgh was just one of the many castles we toured as we made our way through Scotland on over to Ireland.

Growing up in a lower middle class family, our annual vacation was going camping in the summer. We never went anywhere we couldn't drive, which wasn't bad at all. I didn't know any different and didn't care. Even though we didn't have much money, I had a great childhood.

Never before did I think I would be able to travel to Europe for vacation let alone take a 6-week trip through 11 countries. In March of 2018, I took my wife and four kids through England, Scotland, Ireland, Israel, Austria, Switzerland, Germany, France, Belgium, Luxemburg, and Netherlands. It was an amazing time that we will remember for the rest of our lives.

All throughout the 6 week trip, I did not have to work a single hour or even think about my real estate business. Even though my business was making me money, my business ran without me. In fact, the less I work, the more money I make.

Many people ask me how I am able to go on 6-week trips at a time. They are most interested in how I do not worry about my business or paying my bills. The answer is simple. I have an automatic business that runs itself.

DON'T BE A SOLOPRENEUR

Recently, there have been a lot of people talking about the term, Solopreneur. This is basically where someone quits their J.O.B. and starts a business for themselves. The idea of "Going At It Alone" without a job holding you back is appealing but has a huge flaw.

> When you "Go At It Alone" and become a "Solopreneur" you are really just that.
>
> Alone.

Remember the Cashflow Quadrant? The most important thing you can learn is to move from the Employee and Sole Proprietor (E&S) side to the Investor and Business owner (I&B) side as quickly as possible. When you "Go At It Alone" and become a "Solopreneur" you are really just that.

Alone.

This is NOT the way to move to the "I&B" side of the Cashflow Quadrant. All you have basically done to become a "Solopreneur" is move from the "E" to the "S" quadrant. The "S" is for sole proprietor. Instead of having a J.O.B. as an employee, you now "own" a J.O.B. Instead of having one boss at your job, you now have many bosses who are your customers.

Just like if you do not work at your job, you don't get paid. If you don't service your customer, you don't get paid. The reason why I am able to have an automatic business is because I jumped to the "I&B" side of the quadrant with owning just one rental property.

As I build my business, the business get's larger and I make more money. All the while, I don't work but pay others to do the work for me.

The day you buy a rental property, you become an "Investor". The next step is to also be a "Business Owner" by automating the business. Hiring property managers, realtors, contractors, bankers, inspectors, etc. to do the work for you while you are free to do whatever you want with your life.

BUILDING AND AUTOMATIC BUSINESS

Now is the time where you are going to start building your business. You need to put in the leg work to build your team that is going to help you be successful in real estate. In this section, you will learn how to build a real estate dream team who will run your business for you.

Like all other team sports, you are only as good as the team around you. Real estate investing takes a team of people to do it well. I think of myself as a coach that has multiple players on my team. I am the one keeping them focused on the vision that I have given them. Also, I give them the resources and responsibility to do what they are best at and get out of their way.

Being a coach, I am not the one doing the work, my team is. They are the ones who find properties, inspect them, rehab them, get them rented, manage them, and make sure the goals are being reached.

The diagram below shows what it truly is to be an

entrepreneur. You are the center of everything in your business. It rises and falls on your shoulders. If you try to do everything yourself, you will have a business that only works when you do. You want to be the business owner that employ's or contracts with each of these other people to make your business run successfully without you.

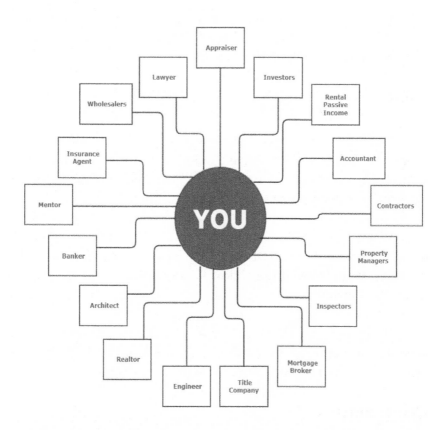

There are many different types of team members you need when you first start out investing in real estate. I suggest getting to work networking and finding the right team members for your team. If the team member doesn't fit into your team, move on and find someone else.

MUST HAVE TEAM MEMBERS

Property Managers (PM)

If you decide to manage your properties yourself, you don't need to have a PM because you manage the property.

I personally do not like to manage my own properties so I hire a PM. If you do decide to have a PM, you must take your time and find one that you feel comfortable with and can trust.

Realtors

Realtors can be your best way to find good investment properties that bring in passive income in monthly cash flow. You should find realtors that understand how investment properties work and not just how to sell an owner occupied property.

When I go into a new city to find investment properties, I usually meet with at least five different realtors and basically interview them to see if they know how to find and make offers on investment properties.

If the realtor is explaining to me about how nice the window coverings are and not how much money it would take to get the property rented, I usually move on to the next realtor.

Contractors

When you find a property you want to buy and hold as a rental there usually is rehab that needs to go into the property. Everything from painting and flooring to reroofing and foundation work can be assessed by the contractor to get a quote for the repairs.

This quote is important because your offer to purchase the house depends on how much money you need to put into the property to get it rented.

If you need to put $5,000 into the property before you can rent it, your offer price should reflect that expense. Make your offer $5,000 lower than you would if it was 100% ready to be rented. It is very important to know that you MAKE your profit when you BUY the house. You REALIZE the profit when you SELL it.

Mortgage Brokers

It is good to have two or three mortgage brokers on your team since funding is the life blood of the business. Without funding/leverage you would not be able to buy a home and rent it out unless you get owner financing, pay all cash, or get investors to put all the money into the deal.

For most investment properties, 10%-20% would be adequate for the purchase of your rental home. If you buy a home for $80,000, your down payment would be anywhere from $8,000 to $16,000.

If you shop around, you may be able to find a good broker who can get you into a home for only 10% as well as get around the Private Mortgage Insurance (PMI) because of the way they structure the mortgage.

Insurance Agents

Insurance agents are the members who will be protecting you in case there are any issues or problems that may arise on your property. Everything from fires, theft, liability, and any other possible issue with your property, your insurance agent is the one who's going to help you get through all of it.

You need to make sure that you have a good agent who knows about rental properties and not just owner-occupied single-family homes. Remember, this is a business you have, and you need to make sure that you are covered well enough.

It is also good to have a general umbrella policy which is an overall liability policy that's going to protect you above and beyond your normal homeowners insurance in case there are any liability suits against you.

Investing Coach

A real estate investing coach will save you tens of thousands of dollars in losses and are well worth every penny. Now, there are some bad ones out there. You know the type. Their business is teaching about real estate, not real estate itself. They may own a few properties but do not have a successful real estate business.

If I had found a coach when I first started, I would have saved tens of thousands of dollars in, loss rents, eviction costs, over paying on properties, missed inspections, excess expenses, and much more!

It makes me sad when I think about how much money I've lost. Literally tens of thousands of dollars... Oh well, at least I am here now and have learned all the wrong ways to do business and now have a successful real estate business.

When you are looking for a coach, keep these things in mind:

- Do you feel like you can trust the coach?
- Does the coach seem like a person you would get along well with?
- Does the coach practice what he preaches?
- Does the coach have a track record of helping others build successful businesses?

NICE TO HAVE TEAM MEMBERS

Wholesalers

Wholesalers and other investors are in the real estate business but may not necessarily want to buy and hold the properties they put under contract. Wholesalers find properties that are usually not on the market and enter into a contract agreement with the homeowner to purchase their home.

These wholesalers can assign the contract to you for a finder's fee and then they are out of the deal. The fee you pay the wholesalers depends on the deal and the particular wholesaler.

The wholesalers usually understand how buy and hold investments work so they will bring you deals that are usually cash flow positive and bring you the passive income you need.

Real Estate Investor Groups

These are groups of investors just like you who can help you with your business. REIG are good to help you find new deals, find creative ways to structure deals, find other investors, and network with others and further build your team. www.nationalreia.com

Mentor

Finding a mentor can be one of you best resource to get started and continue to grow your real estate business. They are hard to find though. A mentor is one that knows what they are doing as well as have the time AND desire to help you learn. Find a mentor that is currently where you want to be and is willing to give you an hour or two of their time monthly.

It is always helpful to have someone that you can reach out to when you get stuck on a deal and you need a little helpful advice on how to get past a roadblock that is stopping you.

Mentors have the experience, the knowledge, contacts, and the willingness to help you in your investing career. It is crucial that you don't just focus on yourself when you are looking for a mentor.

Having a mentor is a two-way street and the mentor must be able to get something from you in return. It would not be wise to go to a potential mentor and ask him or her to give time effort knowledge wisdom into you without offering something in return.

Be sure to think of how you can benefit the mentor as you are looking to get him up on your team. You are selling yourself to them as a worthwhile investment in their time and experiences.

Investors

Like mortgage brokers, investors are the part of your team that will help you acquire the deal with as little money out of your pocket as possible. For example, you can structure a deal on a 24 unit apartment building you find with a lead investor and passive investors.

The lead investor is the one who manages the business and does all the work. Passive investors are there to help contribute their personal funds to the down payment or cash purchase of the deal. Being the lead investor, you would keep a percentage of the equity for doing all the work.

This includes items like finding the deal, structuring the deal, starting/running the business, finding the investors, managing the PM, distributing the monthly/quarterly funds to the passive investors, dealing with accountants/taxes, and managing the managers of the property. Basically, the lead investor does all the work and the passive investors get a monthly/quarterly check in the mail.

Title Company

Your title company is the one that's going to make sure that the property you are buying does not have any problems. The problems could be liens against the property, back taxes, improper recording of deeds, or a host of other problems that could potentially rise.

They will give you title insurance that protects you from anything they may have missed in the search for any issues with the title. The reason why they are not a MUST have is because they really are a dime a dozen. If you find a nationwide title company, most likely you will be taken care of well.

Appraiser

The appraiser is the one that is going to set a value on your property when you need it. You cannot always use your own appraiser but it is always good to have someone on your team that can give you some advice on the value of your property.

Lawyers

It is said that in real estate, it's not IF you get sued, it's only a matter of WHEN. It is wise to have a lawyer on your team, not necessarily one that you pay and have as a retainer, but someone that you are able to call when something goes wrong. Be sure it is the type of lawyer that handles real estate and/or rental property issues.

Banker

Your banker is someone that will help you get loans that you would probably not normally get. Bankers don't just look at your credit score and financial history, they also look at you and see if you are the type of person they want to do business with and someone who can pay off the loan.

If you work with a banker and you are not presentable in a professional way the banker may not feel that you are able to pay off the loan. Even though the property will bring in enough money to pay for the mortgage the banker may think that you would not pay the mortgage. Be sure to get a banker on your team.

Accountant

My accountant is almost worth his weight in gold... I hate doing accounting and my taxes. I would actually pay double what he charges in order to have it done fast and well by a professional.

Find a good accountant that knows the tax law well and will help you save as much money from taxes as possible. My accountant actually worked for the IRS and knows what they look for when considering an audit. This is a benefit because he does his best to make sure I never get audited.

BUILD A TEAM EVERYWHERE YOU INVEST

Whenever I go into a new area to invest, I always work on my team before I even start. Many times, I start a new area of the country without even visiting the area. With how amazing technology is for investing, I do not even need to see the property physically before I buy it. My team looks at the property, sends me pictures, fixes up the property, all without any of my physical help or time.

In each area where I invest, I have a different team. Some, like mortgage brokers, can be used all over the state or country and be on multiple teams at the same time. Others, like realtors and PM's, can only be local because you need the people on the ground in each market where you invest. They are your eyes and ears for your business, and they keep the business running with you out of the picture.

Find the best players to be on your team. This is a marathon, not a sprint. Get the players that will last the long haul and help your team win at the end of the race.

WHAT TO LOOK FOR IN A PROPERTY MANAGER

Your real estate business depends on who you have managing the property and how they manage it as well. If you manage the properties yourself, great, more power to you. I personally do not want to manage my own properties, so I hire a Property Manager (PM) to manage it for me.

I would rather spend my time on the things that I want and pay my PM to manage the property for me. I love receiving my rent checks each month from my property manager and not having to do a thing to get it. All my work was done in the beginning when I bought the property and set up my business. Now it is on autopilot.

Here is a good start to finding the right property manager for your real estate business. Since I invest all over the country, I depend on my PM's doing the job right and the way I expect them to. When I am looking for a new property manager, I always meet with a 4-5 property managers in person while they show me the area I am going to start investing.

I like to meet with at least four different PM's so I hopefully find one, and a backup, that will take care of my business well. The items in the list below are non-negotiable for me when I look for a property manager.

There are other things I look for in a PM but I will not do without these. The only way to find out if your property manager has these qualities is to build a relationship with him and ask many questions.

THE SIX DEAL BREAKERS FOR PROPERTY MANAGERS

Trustworthiness

You must be able to trust your PM. Remember, they are your employee, and they are working for you. One property manager I had was not trustworthy, and I had to fire her. There were missing receipts, unexplained expenses, upset tenants, etc.

Don't put up with a bad property manager. Get rid of them quickly. Like any employee you have, hire slow, fire fast.

Don't put up with a bad property manager. Get rid of them quickly. Like any employee you have, hire slow, fire fast.

I treat my PM's like every employee I have ever hired. If they are good, I treat and pay them well. They are running my business for me, and if it was not for them, I would not have a business. But if they are a bad employee I get rid of them as fast as possible.

Accountability

Everything the PM does should be run through you, and you should be able to verify what they do. I give my PM's the authority to spend under $100 per property per month without my approval. I don't want to be bothered with a $5 toilet leak, but I do want to be bothered about a $500 water heater or a $2,000 furnace replacement.

I review every statement and every expense/income that I receive. If there are any issues or questions, I ask them right away. If the PM is unable to adequately answer my questions, I start to get suspicious of them doing their job well and how much I can trust them. Once the seed of doubt is planted, it takes a lot of time for the PM to build that trust back up in me so I am able to fully trust them.

Communication

The PM should be able to return your call/text/email within the same day, or at the latest, within 24 hours. This is a non-negotiable. Only with good communication can your real estate business run well and keep you and your tenants happy. I have had bad PM's in the past and they make your life too hard to keep them.

I find that the main problem with a lack of communication is that I start to worry about my properties and imagine the worst possible scenarios for my properties. I employ my PM so that I don't have to think about the properties.

If he or she is not communicating promptly, I get concerned because I am worried about my business and that is what I pay my PM's to do. Worry about my business so I don't have to.

When I am screening out PM's before I invest in a new area I expect the PM to be on their "A" game and be in constant conversation with me because he wants to get my business. If the PM has horrible communication while he is trying to get my business, I can only imagine how much worse it would be when I actually hire him to do the job. I have passed on many PM's because of their lack of communication in the hiring period because it will more than likely get worse, not better.

Quality of Work

When you have a good PM, the quality of the rehab or repairs she will do should meet your standards. You should be able to rely on your PM to make the property desirable to tenants and get top dollar for the rent. If your properties are run down, the rent amount will be much lower than if you take care of the properties because they are not as desirable.

Your PM is who makes sure the property is desirable. If you are not able to get the same market rents as the properties near you, look into the quality of product your PM is selling to the prospective tenants.

References

Just like hiring any other employee, check their references, and see if they have a good track record with previous/current landlords they are working for. If they have good references you have hopefully been able to get a leg up on finding a good PM.

I never understood when PM's do not give references. I had one potential PM tell me that he will not give any references because his other landlords are confidential. This was a huge red flag for me.

No matter the reason for him being secretive, this goes against points two and three. It shows that they do not want to be held accountable and that they may not be trustworthy enough for me to hire them. I moved on.

Commission Percentage

The amount that I pay my PM is based on what I contract with them for their services. Some areas 8% of rents is the going rate and in others 10% is. If it is hard to find a good PM in a specific area, you may pay an awesome PM 12% because you are getting awesome service for your money. I have an area where I am paying 12% for my PM, but he is worth every penny.

The biggest thing I can leave you with is this: When you get a good PM, pay them and treat them well. The PM whom I pay 12% of the rents, which is rather high for a percentage, is worth every penny.

One day I thought to change the terms of our agreement once and bring the % down to 10%. After I considered the change, the amount of money I would save would not compare to the amount of dissatisfaction my PM would feel. The decrease would lower his desire to do the job right.

Just imagine if your boss came to you and asked you to take a pay decrease all while you are the one making the money for him. That wouldn't be good at all.

Again, when you find a good property manager, pay them what they deserve.

QUESTIONS TO ASK PROPERTY MANAGERS

Property managers are absolutely vital in this line of business. If you do not have a good property manager, your business will go down the drain, and you will lose money and possibly lose your properties. I have experience in property managers that have lied, stole money, put false expenses on my properties. All of this could've been avoided by finding a good property manager.

Below is a list of questions that I asked prospective property managers when I'm going to start investing in a new area. What you want to find is a property manager that you can trust and can give the responsibility of running your business.

This initial phone conversation is just the start of a long relationship with your property manager. Your goal here is to get information as well as start developing a report with the property manager. You want to find somebody that you can get along with and enjoy working with them.

I learned a long time ago that I do not want to work with anyone whom I do not like to be around. Life is too short to waste it on people that make your life harder and take lots of energy to deal with.

Here are some questions I ask potential property managers:

How long have you been a property manager?

This question is more of a general question for your information. I have had bad property managers that have had many years of experience. I've also had good property managers that had no experience.

I would suggest finding a property manager that has experience managing properties if you are new to rental properties. Remember that property managers are your employee, and they need to follow your business rules. If they do not follow your instructions and it seems like they are possibly lying to you, it may be time to get rid of them.

Like hiring any employee, you want to hire slow and fire fast. Make sure you hire the right person the first time because it takes a lot of work to fire them. After you fire a PM, you need to spend the time to find somebody new, train him, and start your business building again.

How many properties are you managing right now?

This too is another question that is more for your information and is not necessarily a deal breaker. Obviously, the more properties the property manager is managing tends to normally be a good sign but not necessarily. It is just a number that they are telling you and would be hard to verify. I just like to have a conversation with them to see if I hit it off with them and I feel comfortable working with them.

How many vacancies do you have right now?

The percentage of vacancy units for a property owner should be as low as possible. To find the vacancy rate, you divide the number of vacant months by the total months of the year. If a tenant stays in the property for one year, that would be a 0% vacancy factor. If a single family home is vacant for one month, then the vacancy rate would be 8% (1 month / 12 months = 8%).

The vacancy rate right now is a good indication of the market and the property manager as well. The market might be a rough area to rent properties, meaning that the tenants move in and out quickly and there is high turnover.

I have rented in some areas that I would probably have one eviction per year if I'm not really on top of everything. Places like this, it seems like the tenants change homes like they change their shirts. I personally don't see how they can do that. I hate moving.

The vacancy rate also shows how well the property manager

keeps his properties rented. If he does not do a good job with maintaining the properties, keeping the tenants content, and knowing what amount of rent to charge for a particular home, vacancies will get high.

Remember that you are in the service business when you're renting properties. If the service you're providing, which is a home for a renter, is not up to market standards, you are going to lose tenants quickly and lose money.

How long does it take, on average, to fill a vacancy?

This is a great question because the longer property is not rented the more money you lose. If your property rents for $700 a month and the property is vacant for 1 ½ months that's $1050 out of your pocket in lost revenue because the property is vacant.

Did you create your own lease and property manager contracts? If no, where did you get them? Please send them to me so I can review them.

I like to look at the lease my property managers are going to use because it shows me what type of manager they are and what they expect from other tenants. If the lease is very lenient, the property manager may be lenient on the tenant and possibly allow problems to arise and may cost you money in the long run.

If the contract is very strict and rigid you protect yourself from many unforeseen issues and are covered when something goes wrong. You want a property manager that will take care of your property and keep the tenants accountable to do the same.

Just know that a strict property manager may be pretty meticulous and on top of things which will help make and save you money.

What is your late rent policy?

Some property managers charge $40, $50, $75 for late charge from the tenants. Depending on the area and tenants, I usually leave this is up to the property manager to decide. I have had some property managers that do keep the late fees for themselves, and I've also had others that split the late fee with me 50-50.

The property manager needs to keep at least 50% of the money because they are the ones doing the work with collecting on late rents which can be a headache.

What percentage of tenants do you have to evict?

Some areas may have a very low eviction rate, and others may be very high. I have found that the lower class markets tend to have more evictions than the middle to upper class markets. For whatever reason it is, I've just seen that to be true.

In the places where you have high eviction rates, the key is to do a thorough background check on the prospective tenant. Make sure you do a criminal, credit, and eviction check on the tenant before they move in.

Would you please explain to me the eviction process in your area?

Each city, county, and state all have different laws for the eviction process, and it is wise to learn the process as you are getting started with buying rental properties.

Your property manager should know the eviction process and also what to do and not do while he is evicting the tenant. You don't want to break any laws, but you do want to get the bad tenants out quickly so you can get good ones in.

What are your management fees?

Management fees vary from area to area and even manager to manager. An average fee would be 8% to 10% of the total rents collected each month.

You may get some higher some lower, but remember you get what you pay for. I have one area where I pay 12% to my property manager, but he is worth every single penny.

What do you charge for finding new tenants?

This is basically a finder's fee for finding new tenants for your property. The manager has to do marketing, showing the property, taking applications, signing leases, preceding the first month rent and security deposit, and giving the tenant the keys to move in.

This is a lot of work, and your property manager should be paid for it. Some charge the entire first month's rent as a finder's fee, but I personally find that to be ridiculous.

If your PM does charge a high finder's fee make sure it is in writing that you will only pay that fee one time each year from the date it is rented. This is to protect you so that you don't have to pay again if you have to find a new tenant in the same year.

The property manager's job is to find a good tenant, one that will stay there for many years, and not just turnover in six months. One area that I am in I pay my property manager $100 finder's fee every time the properties rented even if it is in the same year which I have had in the past.

If a property is vacant, do you charge for monitoring and maintaining vacant units?

This type of fee is a huge red flag for me. If the property is not rented, I am not making money. And in turn the property manager should not be making money because he is responsible getting the property rented and for keeping it rented. If I am not getting paid, then my property managers not getting paid.

Doesn't it seem like a conflict of interest if the property manager charges $50 if the property is not rented, but also makes $60 if the property is rented? There is only a $10 incentive for him to get the property rented, which is not very much. I stay away from property managers who charge this. But even if they do, I have negotiated some out of this charge because I will not pay it and they remove it.

Do you also market properties as a broker?

This is an interesting question because, like I said, in some areas the marketing can be www.craigslist.com or may even be through the MLS and need a broker to rent them out. Either way, it doesn't really matter, in my opinion. I just like to know.

If I decide to sell my property, do I have to list it with you?

Some PMs may require this in the contract that they sign with you. I would completely strike it out and remove that from the contract or find new property manager. Just like with Realtors who want to sign an exclusive agreement with you, never sign anything exclusive with anyone.

Can I see some of the other properties you manage?

If you're in the area and can see the properties, it's always a good idea to look at how the property manager does his business.

I also like to talk to the tenants to ask them questions like; How do you like the property? How long have you lived here? How long does it take for the property manager to return your phone calls? How long does it take for him to respond to repairs needed?

Do you recommend special incentives for tenants?

In some cases, it may be good to offer incentives to prospective tenants or even current tenants. I invest in one area that snows heavily and gets very cold. So if I have a vacant property in November I dropped the rent amount $75-$100 to get it rented before it starts to freeze.

I have some tenants that have lived in my properties for over three to four years, and I like to give them a little something to show them my appreciation for being such great tenants. They can be a small gift card to Home Depot or Lowe's or even Starbucks. I also like to have a thank you card for them expressing my gratitude. A little gratitude goes a long way.

If I want additional marketing for specific vacant units, how would we arrange that?

If there is a property that has been vacant too long, or one that I don't want to stay vacant long at all, I may want the property manager to go above and beyond his normal marketing for this property.

How do you screen tenants?

There many ways to screen prospects for your properties, and your property manager should do all of them for you. This includes things like checking employment history, checking rental history, checking references, and even running a background, credit, criminal, and eviction checks.

It is also helpful if your property manager is able to accurately judge the character of potential renters quickly. Some people have a gift of discernment that helps in this process, and some do not. It is just wise to listen to your property manager to see if they like the tenant or not and if they desire to rent to them.

Do you give each applicant a credit, criminal, and eviction check?

Doing a credit, criminal, and eviction check is an absolute must for me and my properties. I have been burned so many times because of not doing these checks and have fully implemented them into my business.

A $30 background check will save me at least a thousand dollars a year in eviction fees and lost rents. If the property manager will not do it, make sure that you will have the ability to do one yourself.

How do you collect rent, and when is the rent due?

In some areas, a personal check is just fine, and in other areas cash or cashier's check is the only way to do business. Depending on the area, you need to do what you can to make sure that you get your rent on time, every time, without any issues.

The rent is always due on the first of the month and is late on the second. On the second, if they do not pay the rent, you give them a three day notice letting them know that the eviction will start on the fifth of the month.

Once you start the eviction process, don't stop until you get every penny back from the eviction process. I make the tenant pay all the fees I incur, late fees, and the rent due.

How do your tenants contact you?

This is more for your information, and it probably varies by property manager and even tenant. It's always good to have a property manager that can have multiple ways of contact; email, text, phone, and even mail.

What is your maximum response time?

For tenants, I think an adequate maximum response time from the property manager is 24 hours. Anything longer than 24 hours, you are going to start losing money. Your tenants are your customer, which means they are the property managers' customers. You must make sure they are well taken care of.

If I am unable to reach you, what is your maximum response time to get back to me?

For me, the maximum response time should be 12 hours after I contact my property manager. If my property manager does not respond to me within 12 hours I start to get concerned about my properties and my property manager.

There should be no reason for a property manager to take more than 12, or possibly even 24 hours, to get back to you. Anything longer than that is just unacceptable. Communication is huge in this business. I live as far as 1500 miles away from a place where I invest so I rely on communication.

Taking Action for Phase 4.1

➢ Start building your real estate dream team by searching the internet for the "Must Have" team members. Make a list of at least three different possible team members for each type of "Must Have" member.

➢ Get on the phone and call as many property managers as you can find. You are basically interviewing the PM's because you are hiring them to run your business. Try to select three to five managers that you think may make a good team member. Eventually, you will select one or possibly two PM's that will work on your team.

PHASE 4.2

HOW TO FIND AND EVALUATE THE PROPERTY

His breathing was a little raspy and he seemed a little out of shape. I had never met him before, even though he is calling me from 3000 miles away.

"Hello, Dustin?" a voice said on the other line as I answered the phone

"Yes, this is he" I answered.

"Hi, my name is Bill. I'm a wholesaler of real estate properties and I have a property you may be interested in" he explained.

"Sure Bill, thanks for calling. I'm always willing to look at any deal you may have. So, tell me about the property. Where is it at, how much is the asking price, characteristics of the property, etc." I said.

"It is a 3 bedroom 2 bathroom home in Houston Texas. The asking price is $125,000 and the after repair value should be about $155,000 with $7,000 invested in the rehab of the property" he said.

This type of conversation happens all the time for me. People come to me with potential deals because I'm an investor who buys properties. Realtors, wholesalers, and others are always looking for buyers for the properties they have for sale.

As more people know who I am and that I buy properties, more deals come to me without me doing anything to get them. Even other investors sell their properties to me when they are getting out of them.

I buy from anyone. A deal is a deal. A good deal is a good deal. When a good deal comes to me, no matter who it is from, I buy it. I've properties from realtors, brokers, investors, homeowners, wholesalers, etc. Anyone with a good deal on a property is someone I want to work with.

In this Phase, we will be learning all about how to find properties, evaluate properties, and evaluate the numbers to make sure the deal makes you money. Now the fun work begins, and pretty soon you'll start having passive income through your rental properties.

HOW TO FIND PROPERTIES

We have learned a little about how to find properties in an earlier chapter, but this is going to be where you learn many different tricks of the trade to find good deals.

This business will grow over time and the more you use these techniques, the more they will work. Just like a business in sales, it is all about how many people know that you are a sales man. Likewise, it is all about how many people know that you are an investor. The more people know that you are an investor, the more these tactics will work making you more money.

Business Cards and Flyers

> I buy houses, duplexes, multi-unit
> apartments, and commercial.
> I will look at all in any condition.
>
> **Dustin Heiner**
> 555-4321

Networking is the life blood of this business and the #1 tool for your business is a business card.

If you are going to be a serious investor, print out business cards and flyers. The printing of the business cards is not expensive and is an affordable way to enhance your image and get your message out that you are a real estate investor.

You can put on the card something that catches people attention like: "I **buy houses, duplexes, multi-unit apartments, and commercial buildings. I will look at all, in any condition.**"

Give these business cards out to anyone and everyone that you talk to about your business. If people don't know that you do real estate, how are they going to help you find a new property or even sell you the one that they currently own? So use these business cards and give them out freely.

The flyers that you print up can be made very cheaply, and you can even print them from your home computer. As you are driving neighborhoods looking for a property to buy, you may come across one that looks neglected.

Look for things like, the lawn having weeds that are as tall as your knees, cobwebs all over the house, paint is peeling, and other signs that the house is in disrepair. These flyers can be put on the doorstep or even in the mailbox if it's possible. You never know when a deal will present itself.

Direct Mail

Direct mail is when you go out and bring sellers to you by using an address list of all the properties that you would like to pursue and directly sending them a letter inquiring if they want to sell their house.

There are many different ways to do this, but a good template to use is called the "yellow letter" direct mail campaign. It is as simple as it sounds.

You get a yellow notepad and handwrite a letter to the owners of the property asking them if they are willing to sell their property.

Dear (owner's name)

Hi!

My name is John Williams and I would like to

$ BUY $

your house at (property address)

Please call me at
555-555-5555

Thanks!
John

Classified Ads

Even though newspapers are starting to be out of date, a lot of people still read them and go to them for classified ads. Some of the best leads on properties can come from for sale by owner (FSBO) ads.

These ads can show the motivation of the seller and can give you a little insight into why they are selling and give you the opportunity to help them with their problem they're having with their home. Maybe they are moving out of town because of their job or they need to sell because they bought a new house.

In any case, it gives you a place to start negotiating from. In classified ads you want to look for ads that say something of the following: handyman special, distress sale, divorce must sell, owner transferred, must sell!

www.craigslist.com

Another great place is craigslist.com. This is the online version of the classified ad. Many people are using it today and will in the future. It is so simple to use and free!

You can even use craigslist to find a specific type of the house, like a three bedroom two bathroom home listed for $100,000. You will see homes that are for sale by owner and ones that are listed by a real estate agent.

Never overlook an opportunity that you find by running the numbers. Over time, you will begin to have the ability to look at a property online and in two minutes determine if it is worth your time to move forward with evaluating the property further.

www.zillow.com

As we talked about earlier in the week, Zillow is a good website to find properties that are listed or are possibly for sale by owner. It also gives you the ability to see their estimated value of the property and their estimated rent amount.

This site takes all the comparable sales of the property in the general area and finds the value, as well as looks for other homes that are currently for rent in the area and gives you the average rent for that type of property.

Do not go with these numbers only for the deal. These numbers will allow you the ability to know if the property is worth your time to do further research into the value and prospect of the property.

Legal Notices

In the classified section of most newspapers, there is an area for legal notices. Under this section you will find IRS seized properties and properties that are being foreclosed upon.

Usually, the attorney handling the case will have his name or his firm's name somewhere in the posting. You can call them directly and find out more about the property so you can figure out if this is a good property to buy.

You can also buy properties that have delinquent property taxes on the courthouse steps. Different counties have different rules about buying these tax delinquent properties, and there are many books written on this type of buying of property.

Buying property from the courthouse steps is not easy and does have many hurdles and pitfalls that you must know how to navigate. A big one is that you must provide the full purchase price within 24 hours of the closing auction.

Another huge issue is that more than likely you are not able to see the property before you buy it. So, you are gambling on the deal because you don't always know the numbers and will not know how much money it's going to take to get the property ready for rent.

Drive-Bys

This is where you get in your car and drive the neighborhoods that you are interested in pursuing. You want to look for distressed properties and any others that catch your eye. Write down the address of the property for future research.

You can also leave the flyers that you created or your business card on the door for the owner to see. Keep your eyes open while you're driving anywhere. You may see a property that you want to pursue on your way to dinner with your spouse. Keep a running list of all the property addresses for your research.

In most counties all over the nation, the county assessor or tax collector has the ownership information for all of the properties in the county. When you go to the assessor or tax collector, look up the owner either on the tax rolls or by the assessor parcel number of the property. You will find that the workers in the county office building will be quite helpful in locating the name and address of the owner.

Sometimes the owner doesn't live on the property, so there is a mailing address that you need to get, not just the physical address of the property. Then you can write or call the owner to ask him if he is interested in selling. This is not the best way to find a good property as a deal, but it is a tool to have in your tool belt to find properties.

So as you are driving, keep a list of all the addresses that you are interested in pursuing. Once you have a good list of all properties, you go to the county department that has the ownership information, and look up the owner's names and addresses.

A lot of counties are now putting all their information online, so be sure to check the county website to see if they offer ownership information online. You can even give the county office a call before you do anything and asked them the process of finding out ownership information.

Real Estate Agents

Real estate agents are on the front lines of the real estate market and can find you good deals. There are a few things to keep in mind when you're looking for real estate agents. The biggest thing is to find an agent who is familiar with investing in rental properties and not just looking for a house for a homeowner to live in.

I've had some realtors show me homes who treated me like I was going be living in the property, which is not necessarily bad, just not what I was looking for. That gave me an indication that this person doesn't understand that I'm an investor who is looking for good deals for rental properties. You want to find a realtor that specializes in investment properties.

I have had some real estate agents want me to sign an exclusive deal with them. This is where any property I buy must go through them as my agent even if I find the property myself. I just laugh at this type of realtor. These realtors just want to make money and don't really want to help you.

So if I find a property on my own, I am required by my contract to buy through this realtor because she has an exclusive right to all my transactions in real estate. These exclusive contracts are ridiculous and only benefit the realtor. I will never sign an exclusive deal with anyone because that limits what I can do on my own or with other realtors.

What I do is create a team of realtors that find properties, and whoever brings me the property gets the deal. The other realtors don't necessarily work together, but they are all working for me, finding me properties. They are working while I am doing whatever I want. I do believe that if someone brings you the deal they should be the ones to close on it and not somebody else.

A great benefit of a realtor is they can set you up with an MLS online database that will let you search for properties and alert you when properties that fit your criteria come on the market. They can create an account for you in their system that allows you to login and look at all the properties that are currently listed for sale.

This is a very handy tool because it keeps all of your potential properties together in one place for you to review. Just talk to a realtor about setting you up with one of these accounts, and they will be more than happy to do so.

Wholesalers

Wholesalers are investors who find good deals on properties

and sell them to other investors while taking a commission for finding the property. The commission usually ranges from $4,000-$6,000 and all depends on what you negotiate with them.

They are really good to have on your team because they are doing all the hard work for you finding good deals on properties. They do all the things we just talked about: getting business cards, going to classified ads, going to the newspaper, check the Internet, go through all the legal notices, tax information, do drive-bys, and talk to people one-on-one.

It's very easy to find wholesalers. Keep your eye out the next time you're driving around a neighborhood for signs that are nailed to a telephone pole that reads "I buy houses for cash fast!" or something like that.

These are called bandit signs and are a crude but effective way to find deals for wholesalers. People see these everywhere, and if they are considering selling they will call the number on the sign and talk to the wholesaler directly about selling the property to them. In any city, you will find these all over, so just keep your eyes peeled for them.

HOW TO EVALUATE THE PROPERTY AND ANALYZE THE DEAL

A big concern that most people have when they start investing in real estate is, "What do I do when there are problems?" You need to remember that this is a business, and there is a cost of doing business in any type of business you own.

The goal is to have the income be more than the expenses every month which brings in a positive passive income. When the expenses are more than your income, you have a negative cash flow every month, and that is not what you want. If you buy right, you can make positive cash flow each month from the business rather than having to put money into the business.

I have owned other types of businesses, like a retail store that took money out of my pocket because of the bad economy in 2009. The store I owned was doing well until the recession hit, and then it started taking money out of my pocket. Even through the recession my rental properties kept making me money even though my business was losing me money.

Like any business you need to plan how to do business properly. You need to value the property right by including all possible expense like: property taxes, vacancy allowance, maintenance expense, capital improvements, and other foreseeable expenses, and account for these in your valuation.

If the deal does not make money in cash flow every month when you buy it, it is not a property to buy. Master passive income is about making money each month in cash flow from the rents of the property.

Even though there are numerous other ways to benefit from a rental property, cash flow is what is going to help you quit your job because you have income coming in whether you work or not.

When you evaluate the property, you should always get a home inspection from a certified inspector on every home I purchase. They are trained, experienced, and paid to find problems with a property. Never be caught off guard when issues arise. Your goal is to be proactive and see things coming. When you do this, you have options to choose from. If I become reactionary, my options are limited and more than likely will cost me more money.

Evaluating the Property

What often scares most newcomers in the investing in real estate world is that a property takes too much money to fix up to get rented and to make it a good investment. In all my investing I rarely have ever seen a property that is too far gone to not negotiate with the owner over.

Just about all property can be repaired. It only matters how much it cost to do so. These properties can still be good investments because if the property is in really bad shape, the owner may be motivated to sell much lower than the market value of a similar property that is in good condition. Depending on the price you negotiate with the seller, these "bad" properties can be a great deal for you.

If you find a home is worth $150,000 in great condition, and it is only worth $80,000 because of its dilapidated condition, it may possibly still be a good deal for you because of the value you can bring. By fixing up, rehabbing, and repairing the property you can make it worth the $150,000 that it should be worth.

This is possible because when you put in an offer to the seller you need to itemize out all the repairs needed for the property so the seller can see that the home is not worth market value but much less because of all the repairs. If there are $60,000 in repairs needed for the property, that may be very daunting for the seller to try to do himself, but you, as an investor, put that in your numbers.

This property that you found that can be worth $150,000 but needs $60,000 in repairs would require an offer of $50,000 to the seller because of all the work needed to repair the property.

When you present the offer, walk the owner through each repair needed and the costs involved that add up to your $60,000 in repairs. Show the owner that the property will need a lot of work in order to be livable and/or sellable.

Remember that a house is a product, and a product is only worth what other people are willing to buy it for. If the owner does not want to sell it for $50,000, then it's not a good deal, and it's time for you to walk away.

Never get emotionally attached to any deal because you may make a bad business decision and buy a house that loses you money. There are many other homes out there for you to invest in.

WHAT TO LOOK FOR WHEN EVALUATING A PROPERTY

Structural Damage

If the foundation is bad or the property is leaning in one direction, you need to get a few contractors to look at the property and give you an estimate of the repair costs. Always get multiple quotes when you are doing repairs on a property.

You will have to look at your numbers and see if you can make the deal still work with the repair costs by adjusting your offer price. In the interior, you may have some foundation issues if you have floors that are dramatically pitched toward any specific direction. The foundation may be cracked or sinking, and you also need to have a contractor come and give you an estimate of the repair costs.

Don't let this scare you, but you can use it to negotiate an even better price for the property because of all the work. Remember, you are getting paid for the value you bring not for the hours you work. You need to evaluate each circumstance individually and make your decision based on the rehab money that you have allocated to the project.

Termite Damage

Depending on which part of the country you live in, termites can be more problematic in some than others, and it is wise to get a termite inspection when you buy a house. If there is termite damage, don't let that scare you because it can take up to 10 or 15 years before termites can do irreparable damage.

Like with structural damage, make sure you get a contractor to assess the damages and give you an estimate of the repairs needed to make the property whole again. Also, get an estimate of cost to eradicate the termites so nothing happens again. Like all expenses, make sure you put this number in your offer price so you don't overpay for a property.

Roof Damage

Always examine the roof. You should also get a roofer to look at it for you, and have them give you a roof certification. These certifications are inspections done by the roofer and guarantee the roof to not leak within two years of the inspection.

If it looks like the roof will need replacing in the near future, put that into your offer as well. Set enough money aside for the repairs from your home improvement loan and let it accumulate interest until the roof starts leaking and you need to replace it.

If the first roofer will not certify the roof and tells you that it needs to be replaced, get two or three other roofers to inspect and certify the roof. If they all say that the roof needs to be replaced, then have them each give you an estimate for reroofing the property, and go with the one you feel the strongest about. I do not always go with the lowest price estimate but also take into consideration the person doing the work.

Major Plumbing

While evaluating a property, turn on all the faucets, flush all the toilets, and make sure all the drains run freely. It is common for older buildings to have galvanized or cast iron plumbing which can be a problem.

After years of use, these pipes can collect sediment which builds up and causes a loss of water pressure and stops up drains. If you run across any issues with pressure or the draining of water, get a plumber to give you an estimate of the repairs needed.

Electrical

When you go through a house, hopefully, the electricity is currently on and you can test electrical throughout the house. Go through every room of the house and turn on the lights, check sockets, test the oven, check out the breaker box, and make sure that the electrical working properly.

If you find any issues, get an electrician to assess the damages and give you an estimate for the repairs. Like all other repairs, reflect these in your offer price.

In one area that I invest, the county code states that if a property has not had electricity on for one year, then an electrical inspection must be done by the county inspectors. The code states that the inspection must be done before the electricity can be turned on.

This is not usually an issue, but the properties in the area are mostly older homes that have outdated electrical throughout the entire home. As soon as a government inspector comes into your property they can shut you down quickly and easily if they decide that your property is not up to code.

On a few different houses, the inspection came up that the entire electrical throughout the house needed to be brought up to code before the electricity could be turned on. This was a $2,000 cost that I put in the offer as a repair needed to be done.

If I did not account for this $2,000 in electrical repairs, that money would have come out of my pocket. As it is, I put the cost in the offer price and lowered my offer by $2,000, so basically the seller paid for the upgraded electrical.

Furnaces and HVAC Units

HVAC stands for "heating ventilation and air conditioning." It is wise to have these inspected before you purchase a property because it is quite costly to replace them if it's needed. If in the near future these systems need to be replaced, this should reflect in the cost of your offer price.

One area where I invest is in Ohio where it snows a lot and gets very cold. My tenants rely heavily on the furnaces to be functioning and work well throughout the winter. Furnaces can cost anywhere from $2,000 to $5,000 to replace depending on the size efficiency.

I have had to replace a number of furnaces and have found, like always, it is best to get multiple quotes when you are shopping for a new HVAC system. One company wanted to charge me $4,000 for a new furnace, and I found another smaller company that only charged me $1,800.

The $4,000 unit would definitely be a much more efficient and higher capacity unit, but it was too big for my property, and the labor charges from the company were too high. I went with the $1,800 furnace and have not had any complaints from my tenants since.

Evaluating the Property

These are areas where you could have some major expenses if there is a problem. In most cases, though, the roof, plumbing, and heating units need to be replaced or have a major repair only every 20 to 25 years. So you do not need to expect these problems, but have them in mind because they are the exception and not the rule.

The big thing to keep in mind is that when you see these problems think of them as moneymakers for you and don't rule out the property because of them. If you can cover the repairs and still make money on the property, the property is a good investment. And remember to put the repair costs into the offer price, and try to pay less for the property.

Taking Action for Phase 4.2

➢ Begin building your business buy creating your business cards. With these business cards, your goal is to give them away as fast as possible. The more people have them, the more business you will make. Once people know you as an investor, they will always see you as an investor.

You can find discounts and deals on my resources page:
www.masterpassiveincome.com/resources

➢ Start looking for neighborhoods for you to drive through and scout for properties. Use a google maps or something similar to keep track of where you have been. It may be best to actually print out the maps so you can write notes as you see properties.

➢ As you are driving in your neighborhood, keep a look-out for bandit signs that are nailed to telephone posts or stuck to stop signs. These will be good leads for wholesalers who need buyers like you to sell the homes to.

➢ Look through Craigslist.org to find any properties for sale. You may find investors, wholesalers, For Sale By Owner, or others on there. These would be possibly be off-market properties as well.

PHASE 4.3

THE NUMBERS: FINANCING, VALUATION, AND CALCULATE THE R.O.I.

"What?!! There is a City tax?!!" I said as I opened an envelope from the city of Spring in Texas.

"And the tax is $2,400!! That is going to reduce our monthly income by $200 a month!!" I exclaimed to my wife as she was chopping vegetables for that night's dinner.

"Did you not account for that in the expenses" she asked?

"No, I've never heard of a city tax for real estate. Usually it is only county taxes. Even Zillow.com has the taxes at $1,200 a year. This will make the taxes for the property be $3,600 a year! This is a CRAZY amount of taxes. Apparently it is a school tax for the city" I explained.

"Will we be losing money now on the property each month" she asked?

"Praise the Lord, no. From my original numbers we were going to be making $550 a month from the property after paying the mortgage. So there is plenty of padding in the expenses for this problem. Now, we will only be making $330 a month in passive income. It's a bummer but that is why I buy properties under the market value" I said.

"Yes, praise the Lord this is not going to be costing us money each month. Still, making $330 a month in profit for one property is terrific. Not as good as $550, but it is still good. Don't you shoot for a minimum of $250 a month in profit per property" she asked?

"Yes, $250 is the minimum I shoot for. Well, this is a big lesson learned for me. I need to double check all expenses, especially the taxes for any new area that I invest in" I said.

The expenses in a property can eat all your profits if you are not careful. Learn from my mistake and be very diligent in researching all the expenses that you may encounter in each property you buy. It is better to not be caught off guard as I did with large expenses you didn't account for.

For a good list of possible expenses you may run into, you can use my online rental property calculator. This calculator will walk you through all the steps to analyze the deal and have you input expenses like, mortgage, taxes, insurance, maintenance, vacancy rate, etc.

You can find the calculator here:
www.masterpassiveincome.com/calculator

FIND THE VALUE OF THE DEAL

It is really not hard to find the value of the deal and if it's going to make you money or not. It is only basic arithmetic that you learned in elementary school. You just need to know the formula to put together to value the deal. So how do you figure out what the cash return will be after a year of ownership?

You should calculate your return before you ever make a purchase or even make an offer. This is the only way to make an intelligent decision as to whether or not the return on your money is worth buying the property.

The best way to evaluate the return to see if the property is worth buying is by analyzing the cash on cash return for the property. Basically, if you invest X amount of dollars and can't return at least 30% in the first year then you should not make the deal.

When you look at the stock market, which gives you at best a 10% return every year, anything above that should be good, right? Thirty percent return is actually a very low number, and I have even seen returns as much as 100%, 200%, and even 500%.

This goal of 30% is there to help you in two ways. First of all, so you can make a good return on your money, and secondly, to protect you from any errors that you may have made when you evaluated the property, and it gives you some room to still make money.

NET PROFIT VALUATION

Step 1 - Calculate gross rents, both yearly and monthly.

Step 2 - Add up in total all variable expenses, both yearly in monthly.

Step 3 - Add up in total yearly mortgage payments.

Step 4 - Deduct variable expenses and mortgage payments from your gross rents.

Step 5 - Take your net figure and divide it by your down payment. This will give you a percentage figure that will give you a rate of return on your invested cash.

Examples: $500 / $2,000 = 25%
              $4,000 / $2,000 = 200%
              $5,000 / $2,000 = 250%

Six Ways to Make Money (Example):

In a single family home with a $10,000 down payment the analysis would look like this:

Rent:	Monthly	Yearly
Total:	$1,100	$13,200

Expenses:	Monthly	Yearly
Taxes:	$100	$1,200
Insurance:	$50	$600
Water and Sewer:	Tenants Pay	
Utilities:	Tenants Pay	
Advertising:	$10	$120
Vacancy 5%:	$55	$660
Total:	$215	$2,580

Mortgage Debt:	Monthly	Yearly
1st Mortgage:	$538	$6,456
2nd Mortgage:	$0	$0
Total:	$538	$6,456

	Monthly	Yearly
Gross Rents	$1,100	$13,200
- Expenses	$215	$2,580
- Mortgage Debt	$538	$6,456
NET CASH FLOW:	**$347**	**$4,164**

Since the total investment you put in the deal was the $10,000 down payment on the property, take the net yearly cash flow of $4,164, and divide it by the total investment of $10,000.

$4,164 / $10,000 = 0.4164 = 42% return on your money in the first year!

Imagine if you only put down $5,000 on the property; your return would be 83% in the first year! Try to get that in the stock market!

EQUITY CAPTURE

Remember that you make your money when you buy the property, and you realize your money when you sell it. This is what equity capture is all about. You do not want to buy a property for market rate because you do not make any money to buy the property.

Market Value:	$125,000
Purchase Price:	-$100,000
NET EQUITY CAPTURE	**$25,000**

To calculate the return on your investment (ROI) on the equity capture, you divide the equity capture amount by the total investment to get your return.

$25,000 / $10,000 = 250% ROI!

APPRECIATION VALUATION

If you know your market, you will be able to estimate how much specific improvements will increase the value of your property. Appreciation on your property turns into cash profit when you sell or refinance the property.

Revised appraised value of property: $155,000

Original purchase price of the property: -$100,000

Cost of improvements: -$8,000

FORCED APPRECIATION: $47,000

To calculate the return on your investment (ROI) on the appreciation, you divide the forced appreciation amount by the total investment to get your return.

$47,000 / $10,000 = 470% ROI!

EQUITY BUILDUP

As rents pay down the mortgage balance, the equity increase is considered profit. The equity is only on paper until you sell or refinance the property.

Purchase Price: $100,000

Down payment: -$10,000

Initial loan amount: $90,000

Amount applied to principal: -$800

New principal balance: $89,200

To calculate the equity buildup ROI divide the amount of equity by the initial investment of $10,000 for the down payment.

$800 / $10,000 = 8% ROI

TAX ADVANTAGES

With investing in real estate, you get many tax advantages

because the laws are written to benefit those who own real estate. You will be able to offset most, if not all, of your income for tax purposes because of depreciation.

The IRS states that your property is going down in value, and you can depreciate your property over 27 years, and that depreciation offsets your income from the property. How much of the tax advantage you get from depreciation depends on your tax bracket and your sources of income. It's generally around 5 to 15% ROI from this tax advantage on your initial investment.

EVALUATION AND ROI CALCULATION

Net Cash Flow	42%
Equity Capture	250%
Forced Appreciation	470%
Equity Buildup	8%
Tax Advantage (Average Estimate)	10%
1st Year Total Rate of Return	**780%**

Can you believe you could make 780% ROI on your investment in one year! Try to get that in the stock market, bonds, treasury bills, or any other investment.

Hopefully, you can see that you can make tremendous amounts of money in rental properties, and all it takes is the knowledge to do so and the drive to put into action.

These numbers can get a little confusing, but I encourage you to look this section over again on how rental properties can make you money six different ways. Also, check out my investment property calculator in the resources section on my website. www.masterpassiveincome.com/resources

HOW TO FINANCE YOUR PROPERTIES

One of the major questions most people ask is: "How do you finance your properties?" There are many different ways to finance your deals, and yes, there are ways to buy rentals with no money down.

Even though you see many late-night infomercials with some guru telling you that anyone can buy real estate with no money down, it is very hard to do. I have found that it usually does take money to make money.

The first principle of the rich is all about paying yourself first. This means to take 10% of your income each month and save it for future investments. When you have saved enough money for a down payment on a rental property, you can then buy a rental and then start over again.

The beauty part is the more properties you get, the easier it is to buy more because of the increased income from the rents received each month. Getting rich in real estate does not happen overnight and does take some intentional hard work.

You are a real estate investor, and it is your job to find creative tactics to finance your deals. You can use one type of financing or combine multiple together to get the deal done. As we are going through these different types of financing, try not to get overwhelmed because there is a lot to learn. You do not have to learn all of them at the same time, but it is good to know of what types are possible for you.

Each deal that you find for a property has unique circumstances that may require you to get creative by using one or two of these financing tactics. You should focus on a couple of these tactics I outline below, and try to learn as much as you can about each one.

Try to keep your mind open, though, to the other tactics for financing your properties so that when you hit a roadblock on a financing deal, you can do more research on how to use the other tactics to finance the deal.

The list below is not an exhaustive list but is sufficient enough to get you started down the path of creative financing.

All Cash

The king of all financing tactics is the all-cash deal. Remember that cash is king, and in real estate it truly is. If there are two offers for a seller to consider and one is all-cash and the other is using conventional financing, the seller will usually go with the all-cash deal.

This is because cash is quick, clean, and there are no banks to deal with that could get in the way of closing the sale of property. The all-cash deal is very attractive to sellers because it's the easiest form of financing tactics available.

Honestly, this is a great way to buy properties if you have the money, but it is not the best way for a return on your investment (ROI). Using leverage and putting as little money out of your pocket down to buy the property, brings you the highest return.

One deal we looked at in the last chapter shows that with only $10,000 down you can get a 780% return on your investment in just the first year! Now if you had paid for the property all cash your return would have been only 78% because you put $100,000 down to buy the property instead of only $10,000. The less you put down for the property, the higher your return rate will be.

Conventional Mortgage

Using a mortgage on a property means to get a loan from a bank who pays the purchase price minus the down payment you put towards the property. So if you buy a home for $100,000, and put $10,000 down, the loan you have is $90,000 that you will make payments on every single month until the balance is paid off.

The bank does this because they get interest on the money they lend you. Most conventional mortgages for an investment property require a minimum of 20% down payment, and some can even ask for 25% to 30% depending on the lender you are working with.

Conventional mortgages usually have the lowest interest rate of all types of financing available. There are many term lengths to choose from: 10 year, 15 year, 20 year, and 30 year. The longer the term in length, the more money you pay in total interest, but the lower your payments will be.

See the chart to understand how you pay most of your interest up front in the first half of the term of the loan. In the beginning, only 15% or so of your monthly payment goes towards the principal and 85% goes to interest. Over time, the payment percentages change and eventually meet in the middle.

At the end of the loan, you are basically paying the principal balance of the note. Needless to say, the banker makes his money at the beginning of the note and wants you to refinance again to start the payment schedule all over again.

FHA Loans

FHA loans are loans from the Federal Housing Administration which is a department of the United States government who insures mortgages for banks. The banks basically get insurance on the money they lent you to purchase your home.

An FHA loan is strictly for owner occupied properties and not meant for investment properties. The benefit of these types of loans is the low down payment which is usually 3.5% of the purchase price. Considering a conventional mortgage is a minimum of 20%, you are able to pay a much lower down payment to get into a house.

This is attractive because it means you will have a higher rate of return because you put less money down on the property. Even though the FHA loan is for owner occupied only, there are ways to use this for your benefit of investment properties.

Say you buy one property to live in with an FHA loan. You can then refinance the loan after one to two years to get out of the FHA loan. After that, you can then buy a second home with a new FHA loan and rent out the first. You can also use this FHA loan to buy a duplex, triplex, or four-plex if you plan on living in one of the units and renting out the others.

There are negatives to this type of loan, though. Each person can only have four total loans before FHA will not allow you to use them many more. That means after you have four homes with a mortgage on them, you will not be able to purchase another home with an FHA loan. Another negative is that included in every month's mortgage payments is a charge called Private Mortgage Insurance (PMI).

This is the payment you pay for the bank's insurance on the money the lent you. You are basically making an insurance payment just like you would your car insurance or health insurance, but it goes to the FHA department for insurance in case you default on loan.

Only after you have 20% home equity in the property will this FHA PMI have the ability to go away. That has usually been the case, but there are new laws that potentially make the FHA PMI permanent and may never go away until you refinance the home into a non-FHA loan.

Portfolio Lenders

Most banks who lend on conventional loans do not lend their own money but use other sources to fund the loan from a third party. Even after the banks acquire a loan, they usually sell (for a profit) that loan to government-backed institutions like Freddie Mac and Fannie Mae in order to get their money back so they can do it all over again.

Some banks and credit unions lend from their own funds on properties which makes them a portfolio lender because the money is their own institutions money. Because the bank's lending their own money on the portfolio note they are able to have more flexible terms and qualifying standards for each loan.

Not many banks actually do portfolio lending but if you do a search on the Internet you may be able to find a portfolio lender to help you purchase a property.

Owner Financing

Another way to finance properties is to have the homeowner be the bank. The deal would be to have the homeowner hold the note against the property just like a bank would if they lent you money to buy the property. If the seller is in a position where they can hold the note, you would negotiate with them the terms and interest rate just like you would with a bank.

Obviously, the lender is the homeowner and would have his own requirements for you like a down payment, interest rate, terms, balloon payment, and other requirements that he may come up with.

It is only worthwhile to you as an investor to do owner financing if one of two things are true: the seller owns the property free and clear, or the mortgage that he has on the property is an assignable loan.

The former is where the owner does not have any outstanding mortgages on the home and owns the property outright. The latter is a loan that the owner can sign his rights and obligations over to you as the buyer and the mortgage company will now see you as the homeowner and note holder taking his place.

It's not advisable to purchase a home with owner financing if there is a mortgage on the property that cannot be assigned because most mortgages have a "Due on Sale" clause. This is a way for the banks to protect themselves by calling in the note immediately when there is a change of ownership on the property.

If the full balance of the note cannot be paid, the lender has the ability to foreclose on the property and take the property away from you. Some investors don't mind the risk and buy the property subject to the other loan and risk the bank foreclosing on the property.

I have seen how other investors have done this, and it seems like as long as the mortgage payments are being paid the bank doesn't concern themselves because the note is still current.

Owner financing may be one of the best ways to get a property with little or no money down because the owner is in control and not a bank. You don't have to worry about lenders, underwriters, or any other potential hang-ups stopping you from getting the property.

Hard Money

A hard money loan is a type of loan from a private business or individual that you can obtain to invest in real estate. This term sounds scary at first glance because one may think of a Mafia gangster named "Jimmy the Wolf" with a baseball bat ready to bust your knees if you don't pay. This is just not the case, but you should also stay away from "Jimmy the Wolf" for health reasons.

Hard money has many advantages over other forms of financing but does have some drawbacks. Some benefits include: no income verification, no credit references, the deal can be funded in a couple days, the loan is based on the value of the property after repairs are done, and you can have the rehab costs included in the loan.

The drawbacks are: short-term notes (6 months to 3 years), much higher interest rates (15% or more), more loan fees to obtain the loan (points).

Before you get a hard money loan, make sure that you have

multiple exit strategies so you don't get caught between a rock and a hard place and lose lots of money. Some exit strategies may be where you fix and flip the property and make a profit when you sell the property and pay back the hard money loan.

Another would be to refinance the property after six months to a conventional mortgage with longer terms and lower interest rate. Even though there are some drawbacks to a hard money loan, hard money can be a very effective way of making money in real estate if you do it right. In order to find hard money lenders, check the internet and talk to real estate agents for references.

Private Money

Private money is a loan from anyone who will lend it to you. It can be your mother, your uncle, your college roommate, even the shopkeeper down the street. This is basically a relationship loan because of the credibility you have built up with the individual lending you money.

If you have proven yourself trustworthy and have integrity, you may be able to present a deal that you are working on to one of these private parties and bring them in as an investor. The benefit for them is they will get a higher rate of return than they would in a savings account by receiving interest on the money lent to you. The interest rate and terms are up to you to negotiate with them, and they basically become the bank for you.

A private lender is solely there to lend you money with interest and usually does not take equity in the deal nor cash flow from the property. That means that you own the property outright, and all cash flow is yours minus the note payment you pay the private investor.

The goal is to take the money from the private investor, much like you would with a hard money lender, buy a property, and then refinance out the money you borrow from the lender. Now you will hopefully have a conventional mortgage on the property at a lower interest rate and longer terms.

A way to find private money is to let everyone you know and meet that you are a real estate investor. This can be from casual conversations like "What do you do for living?" You can answer simply, "I am a real estate investor who invests in rental properties that give a passive income each month in cash flow."

Your honesty and integrity are your calling cards when you search for private money. If people see you as someone they cannot trust, they will not lend you any money because they don't believe that you will pay them back.

Home Equity Loans and Lines of Credit (HELOC)

If you currently own a home you may have equity buildup in the property that you can use to purchase more rental properties. A home equity loan is basically a loan against the equity that you currently have in the property. These types of loans do not normally exceed 80% of the value of your home, but if you have enough equity in the property it can be a very good way to purchase more rentals.

For example:

If you own a home that is worth $200,000, and you only owe $70,000, you would be able to borrow up to 80% of the $200,000 minus the original note of $70,000. 80% of $200,000 is $160,000. Subtract the $160,000 by the amount you currently owe ($70,000) and you have $90,000 left to borrow from your equity.

A good way to use this loan would be to purchase a $90,000 property that will make you money each month from the rents. You can now use that money to pay the mortgage payment each month. A mortgage payment of $90,000 may be around $650 a month, and you can buy a property that rents for $1000 giving you a profit of $350 month cash flow.

This new rental property is now free and clear to get another home equity loan on and do it all over again. A home equity line of credit (HELOC) is similar to an Equity Loan but the only difference is that the HELOC is a revolving line of credit like a credit card.

With a HELOC you can borrow money against the equity on your home and then pay it off at any given time so as to not incur any interest if the balance is zero. The small annual fees that you incur having the HELOC are minimal compared to the value that it brings you to have money at your fingertips ready for the next deal.

Partnerships

A partnership is like a loan from a private investor, but instead of getting a monthly note payment, the investor gets equity in the deal. That means the investor owns a portion of the property and likewise a portion of the income and expenses. The equity stake the investor takes in the partnership is all negotiable and should be discussed when presenting the deal.

The equity portion is usually based on the total cash invested from each party to the total cash invested as a whole for the deal. The major benefit with a partnership is economies of scale. All parties involved bringing money into the deal and can buy a larger building, apartment complex, or whatever type of deal you were going to purchase. It is called synergy. Synergy is the creation of a whole that is greater than the sum of its parts.

I'll give you an example from my experience with other investors I work with. Separately, each investor has a small amount of money to put towards a property, but together we all combine our money and have the ability to buy a much larger apartment complex.

If each of three investors brings $50,000 into the deal, then we will have a total of $150,000 for the purchase. On a commercial loan for an apartment complex the minimum down payment is 20%, so the ability to buy a property works like this:

Individual	Partnership
Duplex with $1,600 monthly rent	18 Unit Apartment with $8,000 monthly rent
Total Purchase Price: $250,000	Total Purchase Price: $750,000
20% Down payment: $50,000	20% Down Payment: $150,000

For an individual, $50,000 is 20% of $250,000 and can possibly by you a duplex or a triplex. With a partnership, $150,000 is 20% of $750,000 and can buy a small apartment complex with 15 or more units depending on the area. The rent to price ratio has increased, as well as the price per door has gone down.

With the duplex, you pay $125,000 per door, but with a partnership the per door cost is $42,000. As you can see, the purchasing power of a partnership will allow you to buy a much larger property with more monthly rent.

There is much more to learn about partnerships and investing in multi-family properties, but this might just whet your appetite to learn more about it. The goal of any investor in rental properties should be to progress into apartment complexes because that is where the money truly is.

There are many things to learn from single-family homes before you should attempt to move into multi-family apartments. Start with single family homes first and progress in properties as your skills progress.

Putting All the Financing Together

As you can see, there are many different ways to finance properties, and this list is just a few of them. Again, your role as a real estate investor is to find creative ways to purchase rental properties and work hard to not use your own money if it all possible.

Each deal is totally different depending on the circumstances of the seller, it is difficult to say which method is the best. What you can do is try to understand each method and learn how to apply them to each deal so that you will be ready when the deal comes.

STRUCTURING YOUR DEAL

In the process of acquiring properties, making the offer is probably the most nerve racking thing you will encounter. Do your best to push yourself through it and get the offer on the table. Like all things that get easier the more you do it, presenting an offer is no exception.

What it comes down to is if you are meeting the needs/desires of the seller and are creating a win-win transaction. It may be good to practice presenting the offer to someone you know and would be able to get feedback on how you do.

Try your best to stay calm when you are presenting the offer to the seller but don't worry if you are nervous. Nerves are a good thing to have and can keep you humble. People do not really like cocky or arrogant people and if you stay humble and helpful, you will get a lot more deals done because of your attitude.

Depending on how you structure you offer, it needs to be written in a way that the seller will accept it even though it is a lower amount than they are asking for. The price you are going to offer is based on the numbers you calculate from the income and expenses of the property.

Let's look at the property on 321 Main St. for this example with the $100,000 asking price.

Monthly Expenses	Monthly Income
Mortgage: $536 (5% note at 30 years)	Rents Collected: $1100
Taxes: $100	Net Operating Income (NOI): ($1,100-$175)=$925
Insurance: $75 Total Monthly Expenses: $711	Total Profit (Income - Expenses): $389

For the income on this property, check with one of the PM's you have been working with to get an estimate of what the property would rent for. You can also look through www.zillow.com and www.craigslist.com to do your own research to find the rental estimates.

For the Expenses, find all fixed expenses for the property that you, as the owner, must cover. This would be everything other than the utilities, water, sewer, garbage, yard maintenance etc.

All these things, the tenant will be responsible for unless your lease is written in a way that has you paying for these items. (I never pay these). There are really only a few expenses you will have.

Mortgage

If you are going to use leverage by acquiring a note on the property, you will need to calculate the total monthly payment. You can use my free mortgage calculator to get this number.

www.masterpassiveincome.com/calculator

Remember that you may have Private Mortgage Insurance if you use an FHA loan to acquire the property which will increase the monthly payment.

Real Property Taxes

The County Tax Collector will have the current rent roll for the property. Most counties have the ability for you to look the information up online. Once you have the total annual taxes, divide that number by twelve to see how much money per month you will have to save.

You will either hold onto this money in a savings account or put the money in an impound account with the mortgage company who will pay the taxes on your behalf with your money. Either way, make sure to save this money from each month's rent so you do not get hit with a tax bill you do not have the money for.

Homeowners Insurance

Contact your insurance agent to see what the cost of insurance would be for the property you are looking at. Just like with the taxes, divide the annual cost by twelve to calculate the monthly amount you are to save or put into the impound account with the taxes.

If you are concerned about how to set up an impound account, don't be. You actually don't do a thing other than tell the mortgage company you would like one set up, and they will do all the work.

It will be more common that the impound account for the insurance and taxes would be required by the mortgage company. This protects the bank because they will be sure that the taxes and insurance are being paid.

Homeowners Association

Depending on the area you are investing in, there may be a

homeowners association that you are required to join and pay money into. I personally don't like homeowners associations and stay away from properties that have them. That is my personal preference.

I feel that these associations just take money out of your pocket and dictate to you what you can do with YOUR property. Anyways, this is something to consider in your expenses.

Governmental Fees for Rental Properties

This is another expense that depends on where you are investing in. There are some cities and counties that require a rental inspection of the property to make sure the home is in livable condition. The cost usually is not too high (around $50 per year) but you must account for every expense so you can be prepared for everything.

I feel this is a fee just to make the government more money. I have found the free market to be the best way to keep business honest. If the property is not in livable condition, no one will live there.

If they did, the rent would be so cheap because of the living conditions. Oh well, the government passed the law and now we have to pay. Make sure you have your fees paid.

If you don't the government will never leave money on the table and never wait to penalize you. You could owe 10 times as much in penalties than the fees would have cost you. Trust me, I know from experience...

Vacancy Allowance

The Vacancy Rate is a numerical value calculated as the percentage of time, per year, the property will be vacant. When the property is vacant, you do not make any money. If you believe the average amount of time a unit will be vacant for the area you are investing in is one month per year, calculate the rate as a percentage and subtract that from your income.

For an example: A property that rents for $1,100 and is potentially vacant 1 month out of the year, the vacancy rate would be 8%.1 month vacant / 12 months in a year =.08

The total monthly income for the property would be $1,100 − (1,100*8%) = $1,012 per month income from the rents. Basically, you are subtracting one month's rent from the annual rent total and dividing it by the number of months in the year.

Now plug this number into your valuation to see how the numbers turn out. This is a good expense to plan for because you may need it or not. If you are blessed enough to not have a vacancy in the year, then your profits rise considerably. But if you do have a vacancy in the year, you are ready for it.

Capital Reserves

This expense is in case anything happens to your property unexpectedly like a roof leak, water heater replacing, or an HVAC systems need to be repaired. You are basically saving for a rainy day fund where you will be able to draw money from when you need it.

It is a huge headache having to repair or replace something on your property but you add insult to injury if you do not plan for how you are going to pay for it. I recommend saving 10% of the income each month for these expenses until you save up one and one half of one month's rent.

For the property that rents for $1,100, save 10% each month until you have $1,650 saved up for a rainy day. Remember, this is your money and is yours until you need it. If you sell the property, this money is yours to do with whatever you want.

Now take all this information you have collected about the income and expenses and use my Investment Property Calculator to see if the property will make you money each month or not. I did all the hard work so you do not. Just put in the numbers you have and the calculator will do the valuation for you.

www.masterpassiveincome.com/resources/

You can play with the numbers you put in so you can find the price you actually may want to offer. For starters, use the asking price to see what type of cash flow you will get from the property. Then you can adjust the number down until you get the total dollar amount per month that you are looking for.

I recommend to all my real estate investing students to try and make over $250 per property if I am to invest. Anything less makes the margins too tight and may end up costing you in the long run.

Remember that you make your money when you BUY the property and realize your money when you SELL the property.

One way to quickly find a price for the property is to use my 70% Rule calculator on my site along with my other calculators.

This calculator will take the AFTER Repair Value, minus repair costs and profit you desire from the deal and find the purchase price. This will give you a ball park figure to start with in your numbers.

By no means should this be used as your only way to value a deal but it does get you started in the right direction. If you did purchase this property, you would already have the repairs and desired profit already built into the offer price.

Private Sellers

If you are working with a private seller, you can present many different offers. One would be with conventional financing, another with seller financing, and another can be a blend of the two. The conventional financing offer would generally be a lower offer price for the property because of the costs involved with the financing.

With Seller financing, the owner is the bank and your job is to sell them on how much money they will make if they are to carry the note on the property and make interest from the property.

Conventional Financing Offer

If you go to a bank for conventional financing of a rental property, they will require you to put down at least 20% of the purchase price ($100,000*20%=$20,000) and will give you financing for the rest. Depending on your credit, your interest rate may be higher or lower which adjusts your monthly payment and total cost for the property.

Use the Investment Property Calculator to find your desired total monthly cash flow by adjusting the purchase price. Since the calculator works seamlessly, you can adjust the purchase price to see how much your total monthly cash flow will be.

Since you are trying to replace your income with passive income in rental properties, making your offers based on the cash flow amount will help benefit you to quit your job. There are other ways to value a property but this is the Master Passive Income way.

Example: Offer price: $85,000

20% Down Payment: $17,000	Insurance: $75
Total Loan Amount: $68,000	Taxes: $100
Rate: 5%	Mortgage Payment: $538
Term: 180 months	
Monthly Payment: $538	**Total Monthly Expenses: $713**

Monthly payment: $538 + Expenses of $175 = $713 per month

Rent of $1,100 – Total Expenses of $763 =
$387 per month CASH FLOW!

Seller Financing Offer

You can offer the seller their full asking price of $100,000 with him holding the note as if he were the bank. You can ask for a no interest loan from him for the property and pay him the asking price over 15 years.

He would benefit because he is getting his full asking price which is $15,000 more than he would get if you were to get your own financing. You will pay $556 per month which is a little more than you would pay for a note. The key here is that you have no money down in the deal.

This would make this deal have an infinite rate of return because no money comes out of your pocket. You can find a sample addendum to use with your offer in my resources section of my site. Owner Financing Addendum

Example: Offer price: $100,000

0% Down Payment: $0	Insurance: $75
Total Loan Amount: $100,000	Taxes: $100
Rate: 0%	Mortgage Payment: $556
Term: 180 months	
Monthly Payment: $556	**Total Monthly Expenses: $781**

Monthly payment: $556 + Expenses of $175 = $731 per month payment

Rent of $1,100 – Total Expenses of $731 =
$369 per month CASH FLOW
with NO MONEY DOWN!

If you present both of the offers to the seller, you give them the option to choose what he desires. Plus you benefit because the seller can give you an idea of the type of deal he is looking for. Since the cash flow for each of the deals is the same, they are basically the same deal other than one big factor.

The seller financing deal like this example is less common and would take some work to find. The seller financing option does not require any money out of your pocket in order to get the deal. It all depends on the deal you work out with the seller. The seller may, or may not, require any money down. It all depends on the needs and desires of the seller AND what you are willing to do to get the deal done.

This example is to show that you, as an investor, need to be creative in finding the right type of financing in order to get the deal. You don't know what the seller will choose in the end, or if he will choose at all so present the offers to at least give him the choice.

You can also get creative and blend the two types of offers together into another offer. Let's us the same example property with a purchase price of $100,000 and use both seller and conventional financing.

For this property, you do not have the 20% down payment for the full asking price, nor do you have any money for the deal. No problem! Blend these two together like this:

Blended Offer #1

You need a mortgage for the bulk of the loan and you need

another for the down payment. Offer the seller full asking price for the property in exchange for him to assist with the down payment.

By having the seller take a note for $20,000 for the 20% purchase price of the property you now have the down payment covered. So, you effectively have a conventional note for $80,000 and a second note from the seller for $20,000 and you have no money in the deal.

Example: Offer price: $100,000

Conventional Financing 20% Down Payment: Paid by Seller Total Loan Amount: $80,000 Rate: 5% Term: 180 months **Monthly Payment: $632**	Seller Financing No Down Payment Total Loan Amount: $20,000 Rate: 0% Term: 180 months **Monthly Payment: $111**	Insurance: $75 Taxes: $100 Note Payments: $556 **Total Monthly Expenses: $918**

Monthly Conventional payment: $632 + Seller Payment: $111 + Expenses of $175 = $918 per month

Rent of $1,100 − Total Expenses of $918 = $182 per month CASH FLOW with NO MONEY DOWN!

Blend Offer #2

In this offer, you will have the seller finance the bulk of the loan and get conventional financing for the smaller portion. Offer

the seller full asking price of $100,000 for the property and have him take a $65,000 note while the conventional financing would be for the remainder of the balance of $35,000.

Like the blended offer, you will not have to come up with the down payment because the mortgage company does not require it and you can talk your seller into a zero down deal. Now, you have a conventional note for $35,000 and a second note from the seller for $65,000 and you still have no money in the deal.

Example: Offer price: $100,000

| Conventional Financing 0% Down Payment: $0 Total Loan Amount: $35,000 Rate: 5% Term: 180 months **Monthly Payment: $277** | Seller Financing No Down Payment Total Loan Amount: $65,000 Rate: 0% Term: 180 months **Monthly Payment: $361** | Insurance: $75 Taxes: $100 Note Payments: $638 **Total Monthly Expenses: $813** |

Monthly Conventional payment: $277 + Seller Payment:$361 + Expenses of $175 = $813 per month

Rent of $1,100 – Total Expenses of $813 = $287 per month CASH FLOW with NO MONEY DOWN!

With these different offers, you can see that there are many different ways to get creative with the deal and try to make the deal work for both you and the seller. Try to make a win-win in all situations.

If you find the seller needs to have steady income into his retirement years, seller financing may be the best option. If he needs the cash now in order to move to a new location, then help him get as much cash as possible within your already calculated valuation. Remember to never do a deal that will lose you money in cash flow.

Dealing with a Realtor

These same offers we worked on for a private party seller can also be presented through a Realtor as well. Think of a Realtor as a middle man who brings the offer to the seller. A down side of working with a Realtor in these types of deals is that Realtors want quick sales with as little work as possible.

If the Realtors understand your deal, (big IF) then they may not want to take the time to present it to the seller because it is too much work. Legally the Realtor is supposed to present all offers but sometimes they do not.

Another downside is you may have to teach the Realtor how these deals work as well. Most Realtors are just salesmen who sell a product. That product is a home. Not a house, but a home. Most are not investors and just want to match up a buyer with a product they will buy and live in.

They will tell you about the beautiful window coverings, nice lawn, etc. These are all useless to you as an investor. You know you are not going to live here and you are not buying the home for these reasons. You are buying the house for the cash flow of the property.

It is very easy to get your realtor's license and anyone is able to get one. Since you may be working with one of these types of Realtor's you may have some convincing to do on your part for her to present the offer, and present it well.

It can be that you do your absolute best to create an offer that would work perfectly for the seller but the Realtor pitches it in

such a horrible way that left the seller confused and possibly even mad. Be ready to put in extra work with a Realtor.

Buying from Bank

When you are buying from a bank, it is usually best to present as straight forward of an offer you can put together. If you have all cash, great, cut the asking price by a third and offer that. Banks are in the business of lending money not renting properties.

The longer money sits in a property that no one is making a mortgage payment on, the more money they lose. That $150,000 property they foreclosed on is now a liability because of maintenance, taxes, security, etc. They want to get these off their books fast.

I have bought many properties from banks that had foreclosed on the previous owner because of non-payment. It is best to view banks as a business not a homeowner. Don't be concerned that you are hurting the banks feelings by offering as little as half the asking price.

I purchased a property for 1/3 the asking price because the bank accepted the offer without a counteroffer. After 6 months from the offer date, the bank got back to me asking if the offer was still on the table. It was, so I bought the property and it has already paid me back in 2.5 years from the rents!

Writing the Contract

Now that you have some understanding of what types of offers you can give, check my resources page for sample contracts for you to use on your own deals.

www.masterpassiveincome.com/resources

The Contract for Purchase is a quick and easy one for you to use on your first deal. If you are presenting multiple types of offers like we just talked about, fill out a new Contract for each offer you are presenting.

This all may seem daunting to you when you do it the first time. Don't let fear stop you from moving forward and putting in an offer on a property that will bring you passive income every month.

Once you have one under your belt, it will get easier and easier. Tell yourself that you are a super investor and this is a walk in the park for you.

Don't give up, push on through!

Taking Action for Phase 4.3

➤ Continue searching for more properties on www.Zillow.com and www.Craigslist.com. Make it a habit to be looking for properties every day. You need to learn your market in order to know what a good deal looks like.

➤ As you are going through properties, continue to add to your list of properties in your potential deal excel worksheet. As you find properties that may be good deals, run the income and expenses through my online rental property investment calculator.

➤ You can find it here:
www.masterpassiveincome.com/calculator

➤ Look through my Resources Page on my site:
www.masterpassiveincome.com/resources
Here you will find contracts, downloads and other resources for you to start your business.

PHASE 5

COMPLETION & CLOSEOUT

PHASE 5.1

YOUR 7-WEEK STEP-BY-STEP PROCESS TO ACQUIRE YOUR FIRST RENTAL PROPERTY

In this last phase, you are going to go through the process of finding your first rental property step-by-step. Just think, in seven weeks you may have your first rental property and have passive income to replace your income and quit your job!

Each week, you are going to have action items to complete. If you follow the steps properly, you will acquire your first rental property. For the next seven weeks, you must commit to being an investor in rental properties and commit to following each of the action items.

As I've said earlier in the book, this is going to take time and it doesn't happen overnight. This is not a get rich quick scheme but is a way to build lasting wealth for you and your family. Be patient and diligent in doing all the action items and do your best.

As you are looking for properties and building your business, you are also getting valuable experience that will help you get better at this business. They say that knowledge is power but I believe applied knowledge is truly power.

Take what you've learned through this book and apply them to your next seven weeks so you too can replace your earned income from your job with passive income from rental properties.

If you buy one property this year, two properties next year, three the following year, four the year after that, and in your fifth year you buy five properties you will have 15 properties and have about $4000 in passive income. What if you kept buying more each year and continued to grow your rental business?

Where could you be after 10 years, 15 years, or even 30 years? It is very likely that you could have over 100 rental properties and have a net worth of over $10 million!

I don't want you to get discouraged throughout this process because it does take patience. At times it might feel like it's going really slow, or it's hard to find a property. If you stick with it you will change your financial future forever and be financially independent.

If there are periods of time when you have little to do on your rental business, use that time to focus on learning new ways to find properties and acquire them. Remember that your job as a real estate investor is to find deals, figure out ways to make the deal's work, and get creative with financing the properties.

There are many deals to be made out there and it's up to you to jump on them and make them work for you!

Let's get started!

WEEK ONE
AREA RESEARCH

This week your job is to further learn your market around you. You have already researched properties online and now it's time to get out there and look at them physically. Try to block out 4 to 5 hours this week where you can drive the neighborhoods that you have identified as being a potential source of rental properties.

You may already know the general layout of your city but this is all about seeing the actual properties that you are looking to buy. You need to get a good understanding of the neighborhoods, potential tenants, and properties that you're going to be investing in.

Remember to be looking for the cookie-cutter home that you learned about in Phase 3.1.

A three bedrooms, two baths, two car garage, 1000 sqft or more single family home is the type of property that you're looking for. You'll probably see these in a tract home subdivision where all the properties look similar.

This is where developers have created many properties from one large parcel that they broke up and built many individual properties in order to sell them for profit. These types of properties are exactly what you're looking for when you are starting your real estate rental business.

This first weekend, your job is to drive the neighborhoods around your home and take notes of what you see. Don't just drive the main streets, drive the side streets and look for ways to get into the subdivisions where these properties are located.

Take note of any of these types of subdivisions you find on a map for future research that you can do online. Keep your eye out for any potential properties that are for sale or look neglected and may be an opportunity for you to buy.

This first week has really only one thing to do and that is get to know your market around you. Be sure to do this first week because it will help you in future weeks to be successful.

Action Items

❖ Printed a map of my city and marked the areas around me that I'm going to drive.

❖ Drive the areas around my city for 4 to 5 hours this week to find houses that meet my business model.

❖ Markdown all of the potential areas where tract homes and/or subdivisions that I will potentially invested.

❖ Research on zillow.com and craigslist.com the property values and rental estimates for these areas and make notes for future reference.

Week one is done and you are on your way to having passive income with rental properties so you can quit your job and be financially free!

WEEK TWO
MARKET RESEARCH

It's the second week of your new business in rental properties. Take out your map and list of the neighborhoods you drove last week because we are going to put it to good use. This week you are to drive two to three of these neighborhoods and take more detailed notes on the neighborhood.

Things to note are: for sale signs, vacant looking houses, age and condition of the homes and vehicles, how the properties are maintained, signs of children playing in the neighborhood, and try to find people to talk to in the area. Finding people to talk to might be one of the best ways to find out if this is a place where you want to invest.

Nobody knows this area better than the people who live there and I've found that people enjoy talking about themselves as well as the place where they live.

You can invest in areas that are low class and not maintained very well but it is not advisable unless you are an experienced landlord. If you do, be ready to go through the school of hard knocks with problem tenants and evictions. It's not necessarily a bad idea to invest in low class neighborhoods but just be aware that it comes with many problems.

I know firsthand about these types of neighborhoods because that's how I started investing. If you have the ability to, start investing in middle-class properties. You have a much easier time with tenants and have a more steady cash flow from your properties.

Look for how the homes are maintained and if the lawns are in good condition. This shows that there are homeowners or tenants who take pride in their neighborhood and community.

Look for indications that families live in the neighborhood. Items like bicycles for kids, swing sets, jungle gyms, and other things children play with.

In middle class neighborhoods, there should only be a few vacant homes in the area and this shows that the neighborhood is a desirable place for people to live in.

Look at how the people in the neighborhood live and if they take pride in the things they own or not. If there are rusted cars in the drive ways, overgrown vegetation, homes that are in disrepair, then this neighborhood may be a more rough area to invest in.

If the vehicles are taking care of, lawns are manicured, and it feels like an enjoyable place to live, this may be the area that you are looking for. Neighborhoods like this are easier to rent and you get better tenants. You may even have neighbors around your property that will inform you if there any issues with your tenants.

When you're beginning investing in rental properties, you want to find the worst property in the best neighborhood. These properties will give you many benefits with owning them.

If the neighborhood is desirable, you will have higher appreciation, rent amount may be higher, force the appreciation by the work you put into it fixing it up, and get better tenants because the value of the property is higher. Be on the lookout for these types of properties and make note of them.

Whenever you find a property that is a bad home in a good area, write it down so you can keep track of it because it may come up for sale in the future.

Be on the lookout for people who you can talk to that live in the area. You may get a little nervous the first time you get out of your car to talk to somebody, but the more you do it the easier it will be.

Just approach them with a smile and say that you're interested in buying a home in the area and wanted to know what they thought of the neighborhood, schools, the neighbors, and even the crime in the area.

Questions to ask somebody who is neighborhood

- If they live in the neighborhood
- What they like best about the area
- What they like the least about the area
- If there are any problems you should know about
- If there are any homes for sale that may be good deals
- Ask about the neighbors and the people around them
- See if the majority of people own their homes or are rentals
- If they know anything about a property that you spotted down the street

Remember that people love to talk about themselves so just keep them talking about everything revolving around them. Ask questions, be polite, and thank them for their time and insight when you're done talking with them.

Be sure to ask if they know of any properties that are for sale or have owners that are thinking about selling. Let them know that you are an investor and want to help people with quality places to live.

You never know what they may tell you. You may even learn about someone who needs to sell their home quickly and you may be just the person to help.

If someone has gone through a divorce, lost their job, had other financial issues, and moving out of the area for whatever reason, you may be able to help them in the situation that they are in.

They may need to sell the property quickly for cash or move out of the area and you are there to take care of their need. If you focus on the needs of the people you will be able to find better deals because you are finding ways to create a win-win situation and not take advantage of people.

Your goal should be to create a win-win situation for you and the seller in every deal you do. If you become known as an investor who cares about the people you buy from, people will be fine to work with you because of your reputation. Be honest and have integrity and all the dealings that you do with people.

Action Items

- ❖ Ride through three to four neighborhoods that you will potentially invest in.

- ❖ Speak to at least three people in each of the neighborhoods you're going to invest in.

- ❖ Ask each person if they know of any properties that are for sale in the area

- ❖ Try to find at least one property that's for sale the area and the owners information

- ❖ Search through www.Zillow.com and www.craigslist.com for other potential properties

- ❖ Contact the realtor that you have made a connection with to create an automated MLS notification for you when properties come on the market in that area with your specific criteria.

WEEK THREE
BUILD YOUR TEAM

To start this week you need to get out your list of property managers that you have already contacted and pick two of the managers you would like to work with. You are going to spend some time with these PM's getting to know them and the neighborhoods they would be managing.

Block out at least two hours with each property manager and take them in the same areas but separately. You want to pick the brain of each of these managers to see what they know and what they don't know.

This is basically an interview you are doing with them to see if they are the person you would want to spend your time and money with creating your business.

Have them talk about the neighborhoods you are driving, how their properties in the area are, how much they rent for, the type of tenants in the area, and any general information. Your goal is to get to know, them and the area, as well as specific properties.

Take them to properties that you noted that are potential deals for you and ask them the estimated repair costs, rental rates, and other thoughts about the property. Since you are going with two different property managers at different times, be sure to ask similar questions to each. This so you can compare what they are saying about the property and neighborhood.

Also get bids from them on how much a property would take to repair and get rented if you bought the property as is. If the difference between the two bids from each property manager is drastically different, take a third property manager along with you, through the same areas, asking the same questions, and having them give you a bid for the repairs for the properties. You will be able to compare all three and choose wisely of which property manager you're going to start your business with.

Ask the PM about the rental rates for a one bedroom, two bedroom, and three bedroom homes in the area and make note of the rates they quote you. You will use these rates for your evaluation in the future.

When you are asking the property managers for the rental rates for a particular property, make sure you specify that it should be for the after repair value not as is with the current condition. This will give you more accurate information when you run your numbers to make sure you know how much to offer for the property.

While you are interviewing the property managers for potential management of your properties, refer back to the section on what to look for in a property manager and the types of questions you should be asking them.

A quick recap of the things to look for in a property manager is: trustworthiness, accountability, communication, quality of work, references, and commission percentage. As explained in this property manager section, make sure you find someone that fits all these qualities.

I have walked away from entire areas of investing because I could not find a property manager with these qualities. Remember that when you hire a property manager, you are basically hiring an employee and it's up to you to hire the right employee for your business.

Now that you are more familiar with the area and a few particular property managers, you are armed with more information to help you be successful with investing in this area.

Look through the classified ads, websites, MLS, and for sale by owner listings for other potential properties in the area. Make particular note of potential properties that you are interested in because we will begin to analyze them in week four.

Action Items

❖ Get to know the rental rates for the properties in the area by looking up current properties for rent on the Internet.

❖ Spend two hours with two separate property managers who will go on a ride along with you through the areas.

❖ Narrow down your list of potential properties to analyze and put offer on five properties.

❖ Find two to three for sale by owner properties that you will potentially pursue in these areas.

WEEK FOUR
LOOK AT PROPERTIES

This week you are going to get out and look at properties. It is now time to put all of this learning into action. Be sure to bring along one of the property managers that you selected as the one you will most likely do business with. Have him give you bids on these properties for all the repairs to make the property rentable.

Since you have noted down two or three properties to evaluate, contact the owner or realtor inquiring of the property and scheduling a time to walk through the property. If you have a full time job, make it on the weekend which sellers will be fine to do.

This will allow you to schedule the three properties close together to maximize your time with the property manager and not use up your entire day.

Each inspection should take about an hour and I suggest you use the property inspection checklist in the resources section of my website.

www.masterpassiveincome.com/resources

Be thorough with your inspection and take accurate notes of the condition of the property. You want to do your best to not have any surprises once you acquire the property, so take your time and do it right the first time. Have the property manager give you their thoughts of the condition of the major appliances, roof, foundation, and roofing of the property.

It is important to have a checklist or a guide sheet that is going to help you to not miss anything as you are walking through the property. You want to be looking for items that are in good, average, or poor condition. More than likely the items that are in good condition will not need to be repaired or replaced anytime in the near future.

The items that are in average condition may need some repairs in the next 2 to 3 years. You can plan for these repairs in the future with a "repairs and maintenance" budget that you put into your numbers to be taken out of the rent each month.

The items that are in poor condition will probably need to be replaced in short order and it will be wise to get the cost of repairing it and have that reflected in your offer price. If you don't know what the cost would be to replace an item don't be shy to get a vendor or general contractor to inspect the item and give you a bid to put into your numbers.

With all these numbers, they are just estimates that you are going to use and I suggest that you over estimate the costs rather than under. If you think a HVAC system is going to cost $2,500 to $5,000, put $5000 in your numbers as you are coming up with your offer price.

It would be better to be surprised by having more money in your pocket because you over estimated than have a surprise that takes money out of your pocket because you didn't estimate properly. You may want to get a bid on replacing the roof of a property by calling a roofer and giving him the dimensions of the home to get a ballpark dollar amount for the repairs.

Even though he will not give you an accurate bid you want to know what the maximum amount of cost will be. Remember to always be conservative on the high end when you're looking at these costs.

For all the little items like doorknobs, window trim, door casing, window screens, and any other minor repairs, use your best judgment to estimate a rough cost. Even if you do not account for half of these items properly, you will not break the bank.

These are not big ticket items that can cost you thousands like a roof or foundation problems. Just do your best to account for as much as you can. As you grow in experience you will be able to get more accurate with these estimates.

Action Items

❖ Review the Property Inspection Sheet on my website: http://www.masterpassiveincome.com/resources

❖ Walk through three to four properties with the property managers to get bids from them for repairs to the property for your analysis of the deal.

❖ Fill out a property inspection sheet for each property you walk through for your notes and reference.

❖ Get rough estimates on the cost of any major repairs such as HVAC, roof, flooring, etc.

WEEK FIVE
ANALYZE THE NUMBERS

This week you need to refresh yourself on a couple of things in Phase 4.2. "Find the value of the deal" and "Making an offer on a property". This is very important because you are going to now be presenting multiple offers on the properties you have evaluated and you need to know how to do it. You will use the information from these sections to create your offer and not lose money on the property.

Don't worry about the asking price of the property because no matter what the seller is asking, the deal is only right for you when the numbers work in your favor. I once made an offer on a property that was a third the asking price and figured that I can work my way up from there and meet in the middle.

After I submitted the offer I did not hear back from the bank to foreclose on the property for six months. After six months, I received a call from a realtor asking me if my offer was still on the table and that the bank would accept it as is. After I looked at the numbers again to make sure everything was the same I said yes and preceded to the buy the house for one third the asking price!

As always, you make your money when you buy the property and this is the point where you need to be extra diligent to make sure you buy the property at the right price. I personally do not get attached to any particular property and overpay because I run the numbers and stick to them. If you stick to the numbers and evaluate the property correctly you won't lose money.

Now you can't let it discourage you about the asking price and the appraisal value of the property because you do not buy properties at their appraised value. This is not a home you are going to live in, it is a place you will rent to a tenant.

When someone is buying a home to live in they buy based on the market value of the property which is not what you're going to do. Don't listen to the appraiser, real estate agent, banker, seller, etc. because they are not investors. You are an investor and you only buy properties that are good investments.

I always offer less than my maximum purchase price so I have the ability to negotiate a counter offer and work my way up. You should always know what the maximum purchase price should be for a deal and always stop there. Never fall in love with a property and overpay. There are plenty of properties out there for you to make more offers on.

Now there are times when I do present my full maximum offer to start with because of outside circumstances. If it is a seller's market and there are many offers coming in, I present the best offer because I do not want to lose the property by trying to low-ball them. If a property is on the market for over 30 days then you should have the ability to negotiate the price of the property down.

The goal of your investing is to make cash every month from the rent less all expenses. Use my rental property cash flow calculator on my website to help you find the value of the deal and the cash flow every month you will receive.

When you complete your valuation of the property and know what you're going to offer, the next step is to present the offer to the seller. I personally use a real estate agent to write and present all my offers. If you want to present an offer yourself, check out the forms and contracts section on my website for sample contracts and forms for you to use as a template for your deals that you present.

Now that you are ready to present your offers on the properties that you have evaluated, put all fears aside and present your offers to the seller's. What's the worst that could happen? They say no right?

The best thing that could happen is they say yes to your offer and you have a great property at a great price. Don't be afraid to present the offers or have your realtor do so. Everyone feels nervous or anxious about presenting their first offer, but the more offers you present the easier it will become.

Action Items

❖ Review phase 4.3 Find the value of the deal

❖ Review phase 4.3 Making an offer on a property

❖ Use the Rental Property Cash Flow Calculator and find the value of each property you evaluated

❖ www.masterpassiveincome.com/calculator

❖ Present offers on at least three properties

WEEK SIX
NEGOTIATING AND
COUNTERING

This week you have two things to do. One, review all counter offers you receive. Two, find for more properties to put offers on.

Reviewing offers you receive should be fairly quick and easy since all the hard work has been done already. If the seller has countered with a lower asking price, then put that number in your numbers and see if the deal works for you. If it does, great jump on the property.

If it does not then make a counter offer and raise your offer price by 1% to 3% of the original offer if your numbers still work at that price. This may become somewhat of a dance where you and the seller go back and forth with counter offers. I have had some offers take four to five counter offers before we settled on a price.

Just like in week four, your job is to go out and look for more properties to put offers on. Follow the steps in week four to find other properties to evaluate.

Don't worry so much about finding a new area for properties at this point because the current area you are working in probably has enough inventory to last you a few months of offers.

This is a numbers game. The more offers you make, the better your chances are getting an accepted offer and buy your first property. It may be that it takes 10 offers before you buy one, but if you buy it right that one property will be worth all the work you put in to acquire it.

Do not get impatient at this point. Most of the work has already been done and you are so close to the end. Finding your first property is just the start of a long career in investing in rental properties and you need to be persistent if you want to win this game.

Action Items

❖ Review phase 4.2 Find the value of the deal and Structuring The Deal again to memorize how the valuation works.

❖ Use the Rental Property Cash Flow Calculator and find the value of each property you evaluated

❖ Present offers on at least three more properties

WEEK SEVEN
REVIEW AND REPEAT

You may see a pattern now start to emerge this week. You are going to go out and evaluate more properties that are for sale. It can be either a For Sale by Owner (FSBO) property or one that is on the MLS and is listed by a realtor.

Remember that the more offers you put in, the more chances you get to purchase your first property. If you don't put in an offer the seller has nothing to consider and you miss out on a property. Don't let indecision or procrastination keep you from starting down the path of passive income in rental properties.

Because you are an investor, a lot of your offers will be passed on because of the price you are willing to pay for the property. Don't let that bother you. Each "no" you receive is one closer to the "yes" that will get you your first property. Be looking through all of the ways we discussed how properties are listed and keep looking for properties.

Always be conscious of the rent amount that you will be able to get out of the property once you have the rehab completed. Rents fluctuate from time to time but usually do not go down very much. Once you have an understanding of the potential rent for a property you will know if the property will produce a cash flow for you are not.

Remember this is a numbers game, and the more offers you put in the more likely you are to get one. Review again the section on finding the value of the property so you have that in your head as you're walking through properties. After time, you will begin to see a property and tell within five minutes if it's a property worth pursuing are not.

Repeat the steps outlined above until you successfully

purchase a property. Once you have this one rented and are ready to buy another, go out there and put more offers on more homes. Over time, you will have created a large portfolio of rental properties that will help you quit your J.O.B because you have enough passive income through rental properties.

PHASE 5.2

Rental Business 2.0
the B.R.R.R.R. Method

By far, my most favorite way to buy properties AND the reason why I was able to grow my business so fast is the B.R.R.R.R. method.

In 2006, I bought my very first rental property with all cash. From that one property, I was able to grow my business quickly to 35+ properties with the B.R.R.R.R. method of investing. From that first property, I refinanced all the cash out of it to buy my second property. Then, I refinanced the second property to buy two more properties.

Actually, I have done this method to buy properties so many times, I can't even count. It is a very simple process but does take knowledge and skill in order to implement it well. At every point in the process, there are things that can stop your progress. Things just like what I have mentioned in the previous chapters in the book.

My very first rental property I purchased was for $17,000 cash in Ohio. Even though I lived in California I knew I could run my business remotely without my actual living in the area that I invest in. The best thing about investing in the mid-west was the price to rent ratio. A $17,000 house would rent for $550 a month!

So I bought my first property for $17,000 cash and owned the property free and clear. Once it was in my possession, my property manager and contractors got to work rehabbing and fixing up the property. After about a month or so, the property was fixed up and ready to be shown to prospective tenants.

While the property was being fixed up, I had my property manager looking for tenants. One week after the rehab was finished, we found a tenant to rent the property for $550 a month. This was super exciting! Our first rental check from the passive income was $450 after expenses! This was a great experience and now I couldn't get enough of them.

After owning the property for about three months and having it rented, I contacted a local bank and started the refinance process. My goal was to pull out as much money as possible from the property. This would give me another expense as I paid the mortgage payment, but I would be able to buy another property with the money I took out. The greatest part of it all was that the tenants are the one paying off the mortgage!

Once the refinance process was finished, I was able to pull out $13,000 to buy my next rental property. The monthly payment for borrowing $13,000 was only $115 a month. Since the property was already renting for $550, I was still making a positive cash flow of almost $350 a month after the mortgage payment!

I took that $13,000 and bought another property starting the whole process over again. From beginning to end, the second property took about three months to finish. The property was rented for $550 a month and the passive income was $300 a month. After it was rented, I pulled out $20,000 of equity from this second property when I refinanced this property as I did the first.

The second mortgage payment was $220 a month. With this

second property rented, the mortgage was paid for by the tenant. Even after all the expenses and new mortgage, I still made a cash flow positive of $280 a month after the mortgage payment.

From refinancing the second property, I pulled $20,000 cash out in the refinance. With that $20,000, bought two more properties that brought in $500 each per month. Remember, these properties are in a depressed market where prices of homes are really cheap but rents are fairly high compared to the price of the home.

So at this point, I now have a total of four properties that bring in a total of $2,000 a month. With only two mortgages, the total monthly mortgage payment was a total of $335 a month. After the mortgage payment, that is a positive cash flow of almost $1700 a month!

B.R.R.R.R. REAL ESTATE INVESTING
BUY, REHAB, RENT, REFINANCE, REPEAT

The B.R.R.R.R. Method is the process of buying a property with recycled money. The money is recycled because it is used once to buy one property, then used it again to buy another property, then again and again. The process is basically this: buy a property with cash, rehabbing the property, getting it rented, then refinance the cash out, and then repeat the process all over again.

For various reasons, it is much easier to buy properties with cash as opposed to a mortgage from a bank. It could be that the seller needs to sell quickly and does not want to wait for a loan process. It could also be that there are issues with the property that make it hard for someone to get a loan from a bank.

I have bought properties that needed major work done to them in order for them to be inhabitable. A conventional mortgage would not have been approved by a bank because they only lend on properties that someone can live in from day one.

Think of how much money you would put down on a property when you buy it. When you buy a rental property with conventional financing, the normal down payment is 20% of the purchase price. For a $100,000 property, you would have to spend $20,000 to get the mortgage on the property.

Once you have bought the property and used your $20,000 to buy it, then you may have the ability to refinance the property and pull your money out. The main criteria is that the property has enough equity in the property to pull out your $20,000 plus any other money you would like to use to buy more properties.

Here is a common scenario that happens often:

You find an "Off Market" deal on a property for $100,000. The down payment for this property is 20% which is $20,000. After you pay $20,000, you now have a mortgage of $80,000 you need to pay back to the bank. (your tenant will be paying the balance of $80,000 in the rent...)

Purchase Price:	$100,000
20% Down Payment:	$ 20,000
Total Mortgage Amount:	**$ 80,000**

The current value of the property is $125,000 before you do any work on the property. Because you worked hard to find a good deal, you got the property for less than market value. With the purchase price being $100,000 and the current value is $125,000, you captured $25,000 in equity the first day you bought the property.

Property Value:	$125,000
Purchase Price:	$100,000
Equity Capture:	**$ 25,000**

Once you have the property in your business name, you fix up the property with $8,000 cash. After the work is finished, it cost you $28,000 out of your pocket to get the property rent ready.

Down Payment:	$ 20,000
Cost of Rehab:	$ 8,000
Total Out Of Pocket:	**$ 28,000**

The rehab done on the property has increased the value of the property. The original value of the home was $125,000. Now, after you put in your sweat equity and $8,000 by fixing up the place, the property now appraises for $160,000. You have forced the appreciation up and increased the equity by $35,000.

Current Market Value:	$125,000
After Repair Value:	$160,000
Forced Appreciation:	**$ 35,000**

With all the repairs and purchase price of the property, the total all-in cost for the cash flow property is $108,000. It is NOT $128,000 even though you paid the $20,000 down payment. All the down payment did was lower the mortgage amount. It did not increase your cost for the property.

After you fix up the property, the new appraised value is $160,000. Remember your total all-in cost is $108,000. So, from this purchase and $8,000, you have gained $52,000 in equity from your work.

After Repair Value:	$160,000
Total All-In Cost:	$108,000
Equity Gain:	**$ 52,000**

Most cash-out refinance offers from banks are 80% of the loan-to-value. This is the After Repair Value, not the purchase price of the home. With the after repair value of the home being appraised at $160,000, you can pull out as much as 80% of that value. That would be $128,000 that you could refinance of the value.

With that extra equity, you can go through a cash-out refinance and pull out 80% of the equity from the new After Repair Value of the home. 80% of $160,000 is $128,000. This will be used to pay off the original loan amount of $80,000 and the rest will be in the form of cash in your pocket.

New After Repair Value:	$160,000
80% Loan:	$128,000

Even though you can pull out $128,000, you still need to pay off the original mortgage as well. So, when you bought the property, you paid 20% of $100,000 in down payment. That means you now owe $80,000 in a mortgage because you put down $20,000.

New Loan Amount:	$128,000
Current Loan Balance:	$ 80,000
Cash Out Into Your Pocket:	**$ 48,000**

After this refinance process, you now have $48,000 in your pocket to do with whatever you want. One more thing. This $48,000 is TAX FREE! Because this is a loan and not a sale, the IRS does not charge you tax because you cannot tax a loan.

The Benefits of the B.R.R.R.R. Method

1. You get an income producing property that makes you passive income every month
2. You take $48,000 cash out of the property
3. The cash out is tax free
4. Your tenant is paying off the loan
5. You can then buy another income producing property
6. You can do it again and again and again

As you can see, you can potentially have none of your own money in the deal AND put an extra $20,000 in your pocket to buy another property. Remember that this first property is still making you cash flow every single month.

Imagine if you repeated this process until you get 10

properties. From your one down payment of $20,000, you were able to build the business to 10 properties. This is what I did. Many times over. Now, after you have 10 properties in your own name, which is the max amount of mortgages you can have in one person's name, you do the same thing in your spouse's name.

To continue to build your business, start the process all over again by acquiring properties in your spouses' name or a business partner's name. This will allow you to increase your passive income dramatically over a very short period of time.

As I have stated, I have done this B.R.R.R.R. so many times I cannot even count. The very first time I did this process was with my first rental property. From that $17,000, I have built my business to over 35 properties and counting. The steps are simple but there are things to watch out for.

Step One: Buy a Rental Property

It doesn't really matter how you acquire the property. If you pay cash, take out a hard money loan, or get a regular mortgage on the property, you can use this strategy. The main thing is that you need to own the property and have it in your name.

Recently I used a variation of the strategy on my primary residence where I live. After living here for five years, I have built up equity in the property from appreciation and also paying down the original note. After remodeling my kitchen, I refinanced the property because the value of the home was worth much more than what I owed.

I was able to take out almost $50,000 of which I am using to purchase my new rental property in Houston. With the cash that I currently had and this new $50,000, I was able to purchase the Houston property for cash and got a significant discount. The property is worth about $220,000 that I paid $151,000 because I paid in cash.

No matter how you acquire the property, the first step is to actually have the property title in your name so you can start this process.

Step Two: Rehab the Property to Get It Rent Ready

During the due diligence phase before I actually bought the property, I got all the inspections, quotes, plans ready for the rehab. The longer that my money is tied up in a property, the longer it takes for me to buy another one so I try to make this rehab process as quick as possible.

In three days I had all the costs for the rehab accounted for and the contractors ready to move once I closed and have the property in my name.

There are many things you can do to the property to rehab it to make it rent ready. Rent ready means to have the property in as good enough shape as you can to get the highest amount of rent for the property from the tenant.

Try not to think of yourself as a homeowner but as an investor. You want the most bang for your buck and the most money back from your property. Most homeowners would remodel their entire kitchen with top-notch appliances, granite counter tops, hardwood floors, etc. but that is not what you should do.

Your main goal should be to do all the repairs necessary to get the highest amount of rent possible. Once you have done that, you are ready to rent the property.

Step Three: Rent the Property and Acquire a Signed Lease

Depending on the condition of the property and where the property is located, you may be able to start showing your property before you have even finished the rehab.

For my Houston property, I need to replace the entire septic system and that would take 3 to 4 weeks. Knowing that the ground is torn up and the yard will not look 100%, I am still showing the property now because the property shows well enough and I will let people know that a new septic system is in the process of being installed.

Showing the property before it's ready to be rented is a way to cut down the time the property is not rented. There can be a negative effect though if the property is not in the best condition to show and the area where the property is has clientele who move very often.

For example, the market in Youngstown has a more transient type of clientele that move from house to house in a short time-frame. So there's higher turnover of tenants and tenants are not willing to wait for a property when they need to move immediately.

You need to gauge both the property in the area to see if it is a good idea to list the property for rent before it's actually ready. Also, if you are employing a listing agent, listen to him and his opinion if it is wise to list it sooner or later.

Step Four: Refinance the Property and Cash Out 80% of the Appraised Value

Using leverage is the fastest way to grow your rental business because you were using other people's money. Leverage can be in the form of a mortgage from a bank, hard money loans, money from friends and family, etc.

Once you have the property rented you are now ready to close on your refinance of the property. You can start the refinance process before you actually have the property rented because there is time needed for the lender to put the package together.

It usually takes about 30 to 45 days for the loan process to be completed. I personally want my money tied up in a property for as little time as possible so I start the refinance process as soon as I close on the property.

Depending on the condition of the property it can take 30 to 90 days to get rented. You want to make sure that you have the property rented before you close on the refinance because you can use that rent as income which will help offset your debt to income ratio.

The Banker basically wants to make sure that you have enough income coming in that will cover this mortgage you are now getting as well as any other outstanding debts. They are trying to make sure that all of their bases are covered and they will have the loan paid off plus interest. You can refinance the property for 75% to 80% of the appraised value. Usually the loan will not exceed 100% of the purchase price plus your closing costs.

The way this is done is an appraiser will appraise the value of your property and give the bank their appraised value. The bank then uses that number as the value for the property and will lend you 75% to 80% of that total and will give you cash out.

Step Five: Repeat the Process

This last step is as simple as doing it all over again. Not much more to explain then that. Be on the lookout for more properties, different banks, and new ways to acquire properties. When you do, employ the B.R.R.R.R. Investing Method to your business to grow it faster than you thought possible.

NEXT STEPS TO BECOME SUCCESSFULLY UNEMPLOYED

You are now done with all the phases in this book and hopefully on your way to your first property. Thank you so much for taking part in my book and I hope you the best in your investing carrier.

As you can possibly see, we have only just scratched the surface on how much more there is to learn. Even though you reached the end of this book, you are just at the beginning of the rest of your life with passive income in rental properties.

Now that you have finished the Quit Your Job with Passive Income in Rental Properties book you should have a good understanding of how to get out there and start your investing career in rental properties. This is only the beginning of an amazing journey ahead of you.

There is much more to learn about rental properties and how to create passive income through real estate and www.masterpassiveincome.com is here to help you be successful with rental properties. If you have questions, issues, roadblocks, or even need some advice, I am here to help you in any way that I can.

Remember that all of this is just a mindset that anyone can develop, including you. Just like me, you have been trained all your life through government education about how to be an employee.

It takes time to change how you look at yourself from simply being an employee to becoming an investor. Right now, you are an investor. Tell yourself that every day when you wake up–you are a successful real estate investor in rental properties–because it is true. You now have the knowledge and the resources to help you be successfully unemployed.

I want you to be a part of the Master Passive Income community along with all the others who are in the same place as you. You can ask me questions directly, work with others on the forum section, and possibly even get on the podcast with your questions. Let me help you with your investing and be able to quit your job with rental properties!

For further learning, go to masterpassiveincome.com and go through the blogs, podcasts, and resources which are designed to help you invest in your own education. And it is ALL FOR FREE!

The real estate investing articles and podcast is full of free knowledge and information for you to learn and grow from. Please check out my website for loads of free information on how to be a successful rental property investor.

Sign up for my newsletter where I will send you exclusive content that you won't find anywhere else on my blog. I value your time and will only send you things that will benefit you in your investing carrier. For signing up, I'll send you exclusive content about creating a real estate business that you will not see anywhere else.

Masterpassiveincome.com is here to help you achieve the dreams and goals you have created for your life. Success breeds more success. Now is the time to act! Get out there, look at properties, analyze the deal, put in offers, and get started on your journey with Master Passive Income!

CONGRATULATIONS! YOU'RE DONE!

Let me know how you are doing and if you need any help, encouragement, or questions. I would love to help you quit your J.O.B with rental properties.

If you enjoyed this book, please help spread the word by taking a moment and leaving an honest review on the site from which you purchased this book. Each rating will help us reach more people and help others quit their J.O.B. with rental properties.

About the Author

Since making the decision to be independent and quit his job, Dustin took just 9 years to accomplish his goal because of his passive income businesses. As a businessman and entrepreneur, he has learned what it takes to build a thriving business that brings in monthly cash flow every month. As a life-long learner with a desire to build bigger and better businesses, he continues to grow his wealth and independence from ever working for someone again.

In 2006, Dustin married Melissa, the love of his life, and continue to live in Phoenix Arizona. They both work together on their passive income businesses and they continue to be successfully married with their four children.

Dustin has a passion and a gift of teaching the things he is passionate about. He enjoys helping others achieve success in all areas of life and encourages them to push through their limiting beliefs that are holding them back. Countless others have learned how to use passive income to bring in monthly cash flow with his help.

He has already quit his job and lives the dream every day. He is the founder of Master Passive Income, a company dedicated to helping people achieve financial freedom with passive income.

Dustin and his lovely wife Melissa have four children and are blessed by the Lord to be saved by His grace.

Get 50% OFF the Other Books Written

By Dustin Heiner

Successfully Unemployed

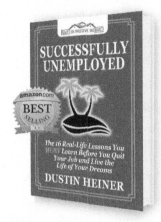

The 16 Lessons You Must Learn Before You Quit Your Job

Entrepreneurs actually quit their job. Wantrepreneurs just wish they could. To become a successful entrepreneur and quit your day job successfully, you must follow these life changing lessons. You don't have to wait until you are 68 years old to quit working a job. Why not retire when you are 58, 48, or even 38 years old?

In this book, Dustin Heiner shows you the 16 lessons you need to learn before you can escape the rat race. Dustin quit his job at the age of 37 and has never looked back.

The lessons in this book are compiled from the stories of many entrepreneurs who have done just what you desire to do. They no longer have a boss to answer to, no longer clock-in and clock-out from a job, and are living the dream life.

How to Quit Your Job with Passive Income

The Ultimate Beginners Guide to Wealth and Riches with 12 Proven Businesses You Can Start Today

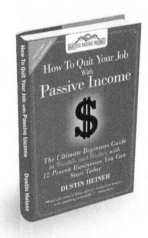

In today's world, we all are expected to live our lives working for someone else. Working 40+ hours a week at a job you hate, for a boss that is horrible, and wasting your life away for a paycheck. But there is a book that will help you escape the rat race of life and ditch the cubicle, assembly line, or dead-end job.

How to Quit Your Job with Passive Income has been proven to help many people learn the secrets of passive income that only those who are already rich know. This book has been designed to help guide you through the process of being an employee earning a wage, to a business owner with multiple streams of passive income.

Lasting Marriage

Discovering God's Meaning and Purpose

for Your Relationship

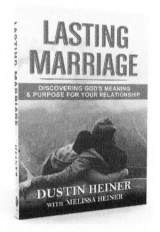

Is your marriage living the true meaning and purpose of marriage? Do you want your marriage to last through all that life throws at you?

Would you like to see your marriage benefit from having more love, joy, and intimacy?

Lasting Marriage is an encouraging and insightful book that will help your marriage grow and strengthen in love and service to each other. You will learn how your marriage can become one of those success stories you hear about. You will be more in love with your spouse at your 50th wedding anniversary than on your wedding day. By knowing and applying God's meaning and purpose of marriage into your relationship, you will have a lasting marriage.

Get the PDF version of these other books

50% off the retail price.

GO TO: www.masterpassiveincome.com/pdf-books

and use the promo code "halfoff" to receive a 50%

discount on the retail price for finishing this book.

DOWNLOAD THE FREE ACTION GUIDE AND OTHER GREAT RESOURCES TODAY!

Don't forget your FREE Action Guide and other great resources. Just to say thank you for buying this book, we'd like to give you the full Action Guide and other great resources **100% FREE**

DOWNLOAD FREE INSTANTLY HERE

http://www.masterpassiveincome.com/free-action-guide

Will You Help Others Quit Their J.O.B. Too?

If you enjoyed How to Quit Your Job with Rental Properties, would you mind taking a minute to write a quick review? Even a short review helps, and it'd mean a lot to me. The more positive reviews this book has, the more these retailers will help others see it and hopefully read it.

Finally, if you'd like to get free bonus materials from this book and receive updates on my future projects, you can sign up for the Master Passive Income newsletter at www.MasterPassiveIncome.com

You can also follow me and Master Passive Income on Twitter and Facebook.

Facebook: http://www.facebook.com/masterpassiveinc/
Twitter: http://www.twitter.com/mpidustinheiner
Instagram: http://www.instagram.com/thedustinheiner

I WANT YOU TO QUIT YOUR JOB TOO!